# THE POWER OF POSITIVE ENERGY

D0967857

# THE POWER OF POSITIVE ENERGY

## Powerful Thinking, Powerful Life

*9 Powerful Ways for Self-Improvement, Increasing Self-Esteem, & Gaining Positive Energy, Motivation, Forgiveness, Happiness & Peace of Mind*

## ANDRIAN TEODORO

This book is professionally edited by Kelly Huckaby. www.thehomewriter.com

ISBN-13: 978-1537222790 (CreateSpace-Assigned)

ISBN-10: 1537222791

# TABLE OF CONTENTS

# YOUR FREE GIFT

As a way of saying *thanks* for your purchase of this book, I'm offering a free eBook called *Abundant Thinking: Achieving the Rich Dad Mindset* that's exclusive to my book readers.

In *Abundant Thinking: Achieving the Rich Dad Mindset,* you'll discover how to become an abundant thinker. This means you'll no longer fall into the trap of 'lack mindset.' You will also learn the power of The Law of Abundance, how to practice Abundant Thinking in your life, the power of Abundance Motivation, 15 ways to be an Abundant Thinker, and the 'Top 10 Secrets' of having a Rich Dad Mindset. This means you will be more successful and happier in life.

Get your free copy of *Abundant Thinking: Achieving the Rich Dad Mindset* at:

**www.bit.ly/AbundantThinkingFree**

# INTRODUCTION - THE POWER OF POSITIVE ENERGY

Hey everyone, I'm Andrian, author of *The Power of Positive Energy: Powerful Thinking, Powerful Life* which you now hold in your hands.

First and foremost, I would like to thank you for buying this book.

I wrote this Christian book, *The Power of Positive Energy: Powerful Thinking, Powerful Life,* knowing that it can help multitudes of people who are currently overwhelmed with negative thoughts in their minds; people who want to change their lives by learning how to cultivate the habit of positive thinking and live a positive life.

Yes, I know sometimes it's hard. Many negative thoughts seem to come into our minds automatically. Do you know why that happens? I believe everything happens for a reason, so here in this book we'll talk about some of those reasons, and I will show you how to turn your thoughts around and live positively every day.

First, let me share an insight with you: Your thoughts are very powerful. The Bible states in Proverbs 23:7 (NKJV), "*As [a man] thinks in his heart, so is he.*" This means whatever you think about, you will become.

So the big question is, "What are you thinking about all day long?"

To answer that, ask yourself these questions: "Am I thinking positively?" "Am I thinking negatively?" "Do I know the difference?" And, "What's happening that is causing me to think this way?"

The answer to the last question is simple: Your thought pattern is automatic (either positive or negative).

Yes, you read that right. The reason it is sometimes difficult to think positively is that our minds are accustomed to thinking negatively. This is passed on to us by different factors, such as our environment, our childhood, the people we associate with, the books we read, the TV shows we watch, the music we listen to, and many more factors.

Our mind is like a garden. Whatever we put into it, we will reap and harvest. If we put positive things into it, in due time we will reap positive rewards. If we put negative things into it, we will then reap negative consequences.

As the Law of Attraction suggests, *like attracts like.*

Our mind is like a magnet, attracting people and things into our lives. For example, have you ever thought of a friend or someone you haven't seen for a long time, and then suddenly, after a few days or even a few minutes, you saw them again? You were probably a bit surprised, and said, "Wow, I was just thinking of you!"

Or maybe you owed someone money and went out of your way to avoid them in public, yet they managed to appear in all the places you went.

This happens because what you think about all day long, you will attract.

That's the power of your mind. It's like you pull in whatever you think about – like a MAGNET.

And now, here in *The Power of Positive Energy: Powerful Thinking, Powerful Life,* I'm going to help you learn how to become a positive person every day. I'm going to give you insights and ideas on:

- how your mind works
- how to attract the things that you want
- how to have an automatic positive mindset

- how to make a morning habit that can change your entire life
- how to be more confident in life
- how to motivate yourself every day
- how to use the power of prayer to get what you want
- how forgiveness can change your life
- how gratitude can attract the things that you want
- how successful people become successful
- how to live a happy life every day.

My desire is that you learn from this book, and that it helps you live your life at a higher level. I'll be right here, to help you and guide you.

Should you have any comments or suggestions for updates to this book, I would be happy to hear them. Simply leave a comment or review on Amazon – I will read every one.

Thanks a lot and *'Have a Wonderful Day!'*

Enjoy reading.

*To Your Success and Happiness,*

## *Andrian Teodoro*

The Founder and Author of "*The Power of Positive Energy: Powerful Thinking, Powerful Life*"

# POSITIVE ENERGY POWER #1: POSITIVE THINKING – HOW TO THINK POSITIVELY

One of the best books I've read dealing with positive thinking is *The Power of Positive Thinking* by Norman Vincent Peale. This book completely changed the way I think, the way I talk, and the way I do things.

Actually, it's also one of the reasons why I started reading books on positive thinking, the power of mindset, the power of our subconscious mind, and the power of thoughts, as well as books on happiness, peace, motivation, visualization, inspiration, self-development, success, goals, and more.

Within the first month or two, I noticed that even though I had already read a lot of books, my mind would sometimes still veer toward negative thoughts. But I continued reading – reading more, learning more – so I could grow more and so my mind could become more positive.

And now you may ask, "Andrian, how can I become a positive person? How can I think positively all the time? How can I be happier, more peaceful, and always calm?"

The answer is simple: Positive thinking habits.

Yes, the way you think is a habit. You either have a habit of thinking positively or negatively, but not both.

The good news is that everyone can acquire positive thinking habits.

# Four Habits to Develop Which Lead to Positive Thinking

### 1. Pray

Yes, you might find this to be a cliché, but it's true. When you pray, you are calm, and your mind is peaceful; it will seem as if all your worries are far away. Some of you may say, "But Andrian, I can't pray, I don't know how." Yes, you can. Praying is just like talking to a friend, and God is your friend.

The Bible says in Matthew 7:7-8, *"Ask and it will be given to you; seek and you will find; knock and the door will be opened to you. For everyone who asks receives; he who seeks finds, and to him who knocks, the door will be opened."*

You may not have something simply because you haven't asked for it yet. So ask God. He is always there for you, always listening to you. Ask, and you will notice your mind becoming more positive.

## 2. Read Great Books

Will Smith said there are two keys to success: running and reading. (We're going to focus more on the reading side.) He also said there are billions of people who have already gone through what you're going through right now. Whatever it is, the answer to your problem has probably already been written in a book, an article, a blog or somewhere else on the Internet. He's right. You can find a solution to any problem simply by "Googling" it.

Did you know that reading great books is one of the habits of the rich? According to Tom Corley in his book, *Rich Habits – The Daily Success Habits of Wealthy Individuals*, rich people have different habits from poor people. Those who are less financially people tend to read more for entertainment, while rich people read more for self-improvement.

Here's how the numbers break down:

- 11% of rich people read for entertainment, compared to 79% of poor

- 85% of rich people read two or more educational, career-related, or self-improvement books per month, compared to 15% of poor

- 94% of rich people read news publications including newspapers and blogs, compared to 11% of poor people

Take note: When I refer to "great books" I'm not talking about the novel-type of entertainment books. The *great books* I am talking about are those books that enhance you, nurture you, and help you become a better person. I'm talking about self-improvement books, success books, biographies of successful people, motivational books, and many other great books.

If you read a great book for just 20 minutes a day, you will accumulate 120 hours of learning in a year. (At the end of this book, you'll find my compilation of "The Top Self-Improvement Books of All Time." I have personally read all of these books, and they have drastically transformed my life. I highly recommend that you read them as well.)

As Jim Rohn said, *"Success is something you attract by the person you become."* So if you want to have more, you must become more.

Also, reading a book changes the way you think. You'll notice, as you read positive books, that your thinking will be more positive, too. That's one of the secrets of successful people.

## 3. Listen to Faith-Building / Motivational Messages

Every morning, I love to listen to faith-building messages. It really affects my mind and causes me to become more calm, peaceful, and positive. When we hear something repeatedly, we begin to believe it. That's why it's so important to hear things which motivate us, give us faith, give us hope, nurture us, and mold us to become a better person.

Personally, I listen to Terri Savelle Foy's YouTube podcasts. I stumbled upon her about 3 months ago. I really like listening to her because of her sound advice in different areas of life such as goal-setting, achieving your dreams, fulfilling your purpose, breaking soul ties, finances and faith, and more. You'll definitely learn a lot from her. I also love to listen to the *"Top 10 Success Rules of Highly Successful People"* on the YouTube channel of Evan Carmichael. He features the Top 10 rules of well-known people such as Bill Gates, Warren Buffet, Mark Zuckerberg and others.

Maybe you've heard the phrase, *"Automobile University."* Many successful people grow their minds by listening to great audios during their travel time to and from work every day. They use the time spent in their automobile to put positive, faith-building, motivational, inspirational thoughts into their minds.

Make sure you have something to listen to during your commute that can inspire you, motivate you, encourage you, and build your faith. You'll notice your mind becoming more positive day by day.

## 4. Say Positive Words / Affirmations

One of the most effective ways to train your mind to stay in a state of positive thinking is to always speak positive words, or affirmations, to yourself. Your words are very powerful, so always use them for good.

The Bible says in Proverbs 18:21 (KJV), *"Death and life are in the power of the tongue; and they that love it shall eat the fruit thereof."*

One of the most powerful affirmations that I've encountered is found in Philippians 4:13 (NKJV), "*I can do all things through Christ who strengthens me.*"

Yes, that one alone will drastically change your life if you say it more often.

Here are a few more of the affirmations I really like saying out loud:

*"Every day, in every way, I'm getting better and better and better."*

*"Every day, in every way, I'm getting stronger and stronger and stronger."*

*"Every day, in every way, I'm getting healthier and healthier and healthier."*

*"Today is a brand new day. Today is going to be a great, great, great day."*

*"I am optimistic. I look at the bright side of life. I create my own opportunities and take action to make things happen. So it is."*

*"I am a champion. I am born to win, and I am destined to succeed. So it is."*

*"I am special and unique; a priceless treasure on the face of the earth. I am one of a kind, the rarest thing in creation. So it is."*

*"I am happy, healthy, and prosperous."*

Those are just some of the affirmations I use in my life. You can incorporate these, and more, into your life.

Once again, friend, use your words to empower, to motivate, to inspire, and to bless yourself and others. Inject positive words into every conversation. Stay positive – think positive.

Those are the things we can do to develop the habit of positive thinking. I'm sure, if you start doing them, within a month you will become a more peaceful, calm, happy, and positive person.

Again, as a recap, here are the four habits we can develop which lead to positive thinking:

1. Pray

2. Read Great Books

3. Listen to Faith-Building / Motivational Messages

4. Say Positive Words / Affirmations

I have incorporated these habits into my life, and my mindset is now tuned into a more positive vibration. You will notice you are happier the moment you begin practicing these four amazing habits. So remember: Think positively at all times. By changing our thinking, we change our lives.

# POSITIVE ENERGY POWER #2: CONFIDENCE – 7 WAYS TO GAIN CONFIDENCE AND INCREASE SELF-ESTEEM

What is one of the most common problems in the world today? Low self-esteem (or low confidence).

Yes, this one aspect of life has a major impact on achieving success and attaining our goals. But why do you think most people have low self-esteem? And have you ever wondered, "How do I gain confidence and self-esteem?"

Maybe it was in the past, or maybe you are still experiencing it – that feeling of *Why is this happening to me?* – that feeling of anxiety, low self-esteem, or low confidence in yourself.

Why? Well, I don't have the specific answer for the question 'why' but I do have an answer to that loving question 'how'.

# Let's Tackle 7 Ways to Gain Confidence and Self-Esteem:

### 1. Take Action

Have you ever noticed when you want to do something which you think is difficult, it can be very hard to get started? You procrastinate because your mind thinks of so many other things you need to do first. At the same time, the longer you put it off, the more your confidence shrinks and your self-esteem lowers. Why?

Because your subconscious mind is continually telling you that you have this big, difficult task to do, and until you complete it, you feel an emptiness within which lowers your energy.

Did you know that once you do those bigger tasks, and complete them, you will feel lighter? The weight will be lifted from your shoulders, and you will be able to say, "Wow, I'm very proud of myself! I have completed it." "Yes! Success!" "Completed and done – let's celebrate!"

That sense of completeness, of relief, will definitely increase your confidence and self-esteem.

So, if you're struggling to get that big task done, do something about it. Take action; break it up into little pieces. Do it bite by bite, one thing at a time. Focus on just one small task before moving on to the next one. Feel the satisfaction of each accomplishment you've made, and be proud of yourself.

Little by little, your confidence will grow, and your self-esteem will go up.

The most difficult part of accomplishing anything is the *beginning*. But once you start, you will realize you're *in the flow* and ready to encounter anything that comes your way. You are now unstoppable.

So, friend, always take action *immediately* when you need to do a task. You will see your confidence and self-esteem increase as you take more and more action.

## 2. Groom Yourself; Dress Nicely

When you look at yourself in the mirror, do you like what you see? Do you feel your hairstyle is appropriate, and that you look nice?

Have you ever noticed when you get dressed up that your attitude immediately changes? That your confidence is lifted a bit higher? That your self-esteem is rising?

Studies have shown that what you wear affects your confidence.

Therefore, to feel more confident and boost your self-esteem, get into the habit of dressing nicely. Even at home, try to dress nicely: style your hair, wear clothes that make you feel good about yourself, splash on some cologne/perfume that you like, smile, hold your head up high, pull your shoulders back, and feel handsome/beautiful.

Every day, friend, groom yourself and dress nicely. You will notice your confidence growing and your self-esteem increasing every single day.

### 3. Be with Positive People

Have you ever been in a conversation where all of the topics seem to drain your energy because they are mostly negative? How do you feel after having conversations such as these with your friends? Are these conversations nurturing? Do they lift you, or anyone else, up?

The answer is obviously no; they drain your energy. If you want to gain confidence and self-esteem, you need to be around positive people. You must consciously choose to be with people who nurture you, encourage you, and believe in you.

You can join a local Christian church where people are encouraging, accommodating, and supportive of you. A solid Christian church will show you love, hope, and encouragement. The members will not judge you but love you for who you are.

Another option is to join a community online. These communities are often very accommodating, helpful, and friendly.

I've been in one particular online community for about a month now. In this community, I'm not only learning a lot about online business, but I'm also getting lots of useful training and encountering wonderful people every day; people who are there to help me, support me with my endeavors and encourage me as we travel this journey together.

They are people who are willing to help, true people who are always there to support you. If you find yourself alone, try joining an online community. There you will not only learn a lot, but you will also meet some wonderful people along the way who will guide you, help you, nurture you, and encourage you every single day.

So, friend, be with positive people. Be part of a community and gain more confidence and self-esteem along the way.

## 4. Speak Up

Have you ever been at a conference or seminar, where the speaker finishes speaking and asks the audience if there are any questions, and everyone looks down to avoid being called on? Or, maybe you've been in a conversation with a group of people, and everybody is talking and sharing while you're only listening and not sharing or speaking up?

While there is nothing wrong with being quiet, always remember it is the people who ask for things who receive them. It's the people who speak up. It's the people who make their voices heard who make a difference. It's the people who speak up who usually act on their ideas. They aren't necessarily the most self-confident or well-educated people, but they're the brave people. They're the ones who overcame their shyness and fears and spoke anyway – those who felt the fear and acted anyway.

When you're afraid of speaking up, always remember this: You are a human being like everyone else. Everyone has their own worries, concerns, and fears. You are not that much different from anyone else. So, be human; be yourself. Never be afraid of people, or what they say about you.

Life is short, and you only have one life to live. Speak up – always – this is one of the most important things you can do to improve your confidence and self-esteem.

Whenever you're at a conference or seminar, be the first to speak up and ask a question. Whenever you're in a group, and you're brainstorming, be the first to suggest an idea. Whenever you meet someone you know, be the first to start the conversation. Whenever you feel you need to talk to a stranger, be the first to act.

Friend, there's power – and confidence – in being the first to speak. Afterward, you can relax and bask in the knowledge that you took that first step and spoke up.

Always speak up. Remember that you are important. Believe in yourself. You are wonderfully created by our Almighty God, so never be afraid to speak up.

Let your voice be heard. Hold your head high. Let your confidence and self-esteem be apparent to everyone. Speak up!

## 5. Start Speaking Positive Words to Yourself

Read this out loud: "I love you."

Did you hear that? Keep reading.

> "I'm so proud of you."

> "I believe in you."

> "You're awesome."

> "You're great."

> "You're incredible."

> "You're amazing."

Did you hear your voice saying those words? Those words *must* come from you, from inside you.

If you're not hearing them, then *start* saying them – *now*!

Always say positive things about and to yourself. You might not realize it, but you are always talking to yourself. Every minute, every second, every moment. Conversations are always happening in your head. Your *mind* is always talking, so be aware of what you say to yourself.

Always say something *positive* about yourself. Things like:

"You are beautiful/handsome."

"You can do it."

"You are kind and generous."

"You are a champion."

"You are special and unique."

"You are magnificent."

"You are happy, healthy, and prosperous."

"You are an amazing child of God."

"You are wonderful."

Start repeating positive things about yourself – every day, every hour, every minute, and every second.

Words are powerful. Utilize the power of your words; speak positively. Speak life!

## 6. Prepare and Plan

How else can you gain confidence and self-esteem? Through preparation and planning.

Preparation is key to building your confidence and self-esteem.

Have you ever been at a job interview and found yourself speechless halfway through because you didn't know what to say? Or have you ever taken an exam when you didn't have time to review the material? Or maybe you've had to give a report and found yourself stuttering through it because you didn't have time to prepare.

Planning is another key to building your confidence and self-esteem.

Yes, preparation and planning ahead of time are absolutely essential if you want to gain confidence and self-esteem; they can give you the gift of time. A little time spent preparing and planning today can give us free time tomorrow.

Some of you may be asking, "But Andrian, how can I prepare and plan?"

To prepare and plan, be strategic. First, list all the things you need to accomplish. Schedule them – hour by hour.

Do this for the whole day, including meal and break times. For example:

> 5:30-6:00 AM – Daily devotions (Bible reading and prayer)

6:00-6:45 AM – Breakfast, prep for day (bathing, getting dressed, etc.)

6:45-7:30 AM – Daily commute to work (listen to faith-building podcasts)

Keep going like this until your bedtime – and schedule your bedtime, too. Scheduling makes you more likely to do things because it lets your brain know there is a time to do each task.

Also, you will notice your tasks for the day are easier to remember and follow once you've written them down. It doesn't take long – you can make a schedule for your whole day in about 5 minutes.

You want to control your life? Control your time. Your life is your time. If you want to plan your life, plan your time.

Friend, when you are prepared and have plans, then you will gain more confidence and self-esteem. At the same time, you will have more peace within, and you'll feel you are really in control of your life.

### 7. Have Faith in God

The Bible says in 2 Chronicles 32:8, "'*With him is only the arm of flesh, but with us is the LORD our God to help us and to fight our battles.' And the people **gained confidence** from what Hezekiah the king of Judah said.*"

Without God, we can do nothing. But with God, we can do everything. One of the best antidotes to low self-esteem and low self-confidence is this: *Faith in God.*

Yes, one of the most powerful things which you can have in life is *faith in God*. When you have faith in God, you ultimately feel you can do all things.

There are many encouraging, motivating, inspiring, and loving words in the Bible. When we apply them to our lives, they make a huge impact. Here are just a few of those verses:

*"What, then, shall we say in response to these things? If God is for us, who can be against us?" (Romans 8:31)*

*"So do not fear, for I am with you;*
*do not be dismayed, for I am your God.*
*I will strengthen you and help you;*
*I will uphold you with my righteous right hand." (Isaiah 41:10)*

*"..but those who hope in the Lord*
*will renew their strength.*
*They will soar on wings like eagles;*
*they will run and not grow weary,*
*they will walk and not be faint." (Isaiah 40:31)*

The Bible is filled with love, joy, peace, happiness, faith, prosperity, and confidence, in abundance!

If you want to fill your life with confidence and high self-esteem, then have faith in God. Be filled with His Word.

God's words are life. They are alive. God can sustain you, and move mountains for you. Always have faith in God.

Start your day by reading the Bible, even if only for 5 to 10 minutes each a day. Talk to God first before anything else; release your worries to Him. Pray for good health, protection, love, joy, peace, happiness, enthusiasm, and abundance, for you and your family.

Do this every single day, and you will discover the secret to gaining confidence and self-esteem: *Faith in God*.

Let's recap once again, friend, the seven ways to increase self-confidence and gain self-esteem:

- Take Action

- Groom Yourself; Dress Nicely

- Be with Positive People

- Speak Up

- Start Speaking Positive Words to Yourself

- Prepare and Plan

- Have Faith in God

These seven strategies and tips will increase your confidence and self-esteem when you do them daily. They are truly amazing.

Before I end this chapter, I would like to share with you a beautiful quote by Joe Namath:

*"When you have confidence, you can have a lot of fun. And when you have fun, you can do amazing things."*

Friend, always remember, you can do amazing things!

# POSITIVE ENERGY POWER #3: MORNING HABITS – TOP 5 SECRETS OF SUCCESSFUL PEOPLE

*"If today were the last day of my life, would I want to do what I'm about to do today?"*

This is the question Steve Jobs asked himself every morning. As you can see, this question gives meaning to life. Or, maybe you've asked the question, "If today were my last day on earth, how would I spend it?"

For me, this is an exciting question. Pondering this simple question makes me realize the things which I need to prioritize.

Now, here is my question for you: Are you doing what you really want to do, or are you being controlled by your circumstances and the people around you?

This simple morning habit of Steve Jobs, the co-founder of Apple, changed his life; he became one of the most successful people in the world.

Morning habits. Can they really change your life? Are there specific ones which successful people do every day? What are the morning habits, or morning routines, of successful people? Do they really have common habits which have helped them achieve success in life?

These are the questions that we will answer in this chapter. By the end, I hope you will be filled with so much insight and wisdom about the morning habits of successful people that you desire to apply them to your life.

Are you ready? Then, hold on tight! We're about to embark on a new journey that will lead to the paradise of success.

# Here are the Top 5 Morning Routines of Successful People:

## 1. Successful People Get Up Early (Opportunity Clock)

Did you know that successful people are early risers? You may be asking, "Andrian, what do you mean by that?"

I mean, successful people get up early, as in "early in the morning."

Here are a few examples:

Jack Dorsey, co-founder of Twitter, wakes up at 5:30 in the morning.

Bob Igor, Disney CEO, gets up at 4:30 each morning.

Richard Branson, founder and chairman of the Virgin Group, wakes up at 5:45 every morning.

Tim Cook, Apple CEO, wakes up at 3:45 every morning (Yes, every morning!)

These are only a few of the successful people who have shared their morning routines.

This may lead you to ask, "Andrian, why are they doing that? Why are they getting up so early when it's so nice to sleep?" I believe they are doing this because successful people have a different mindset.

They know that willpower is strongest in the morning. They know 30 minutes to an hour of time for themselves in the morning makes a big difference in their lives.

Now, I would like to introduce you to the term "*opportunity clock*" which Zig Ziglar coined a few years ago.

He said that instead of using the term "alarm clock" (which is negative), we should replace the phrase with "*opportunity clock*" (which is positive).

This way, once the "*opportunity clock*" is ticking, our mindset is thinking in the positive direction. This will give us a boost to get up and go, to get on with our day full of "opportunities."

Well, I say Zig is right. By changing the words, phrases, and terms we use, we can change our lives.

Successful people see opportunities in every day. They grab those opportunities and become better, happier, stronger, and what they want to be. That's why they are successful.

Not only that, but they get up early because they do "*something*" early. Let's look more at this "*something*" that they do early in the morning.

But first, friend, let me reiterate the importance of changing your vocabulary and using the phrase "opportunity clock" each day. By doing so, you will eventually see changes in your daily life.

As you can see, we started the morning habits of successful people by introducing the concept of getting up early. Why? Because they are connected to each other.

Now, we will dig into those morning rituals to see exactly what the "*something*" is that successful people do when they get up early.

## 2. Successful People Exercise

Did you know successful people really do work out, especially in the morning? That's one of the things they do when they get up early.

Here are a few examples:

Oprah Winfrey does 45 minutes of cardio exercise six mornings a week, plus four or five strength training sessions which include crunches and stretching.

Richard Branson gets an additional four hours of productivity by working out. His physical activities include swimming, Bikram yoga, rock climbing, running, and weightlifting.

Anna Wintour, the famed editor-in-chief of American Vogue, gets up every day at 5:45 AM to play tennis.

And lastly, former President Barack Obama works out 45 minutes a day, 6 days a week. He's also been known to play basketball on courts in federal buildings around Washington.

These are just a few of the most successful people in the world who make time for physical exercise every day.

So again, friend, get up early in the morning, while your willpower is at its strongest, and do your workout and exercise routines. This one habit can truly make you physically healthy, productive and happy for the whole day.

### 3. Successful People Have a Quiet Time

Successful people have a quiet time in the morning. They do meditations, prayers, mindfulness, or breathing exercises. They do it to clear their minds early in the morning, so that they are more relaxed, calmer, and happier, which allows them to tackle the rest of their day.

Having a quiet time in the morning is like filling yourself up with unlimited fuel for the day ahead of you. It gives you energy, makes you peaceful and calm, helps you to have a right perspective, and tunes your day.

Here are a few examples of successful people who do meditations or have a quiet time in the morning:

After a meditation in Iowa last year, Oprah said, *"I walked away feeling fuller than when I'd come in. Full of hope, a sense of contentment, and deep joy. Knowing for sure that even in the daily craziness that bombards us from every direction, there is -- still -- the constancy of stillness. Only from that space can you create your best work and your best life."*

Russell Simmons, founder of GlobalGrind.com also meditates. *"You don't have to believe in meditation for it to work,"* Simmons wrote in a Huffington Post blog. *"You just have to take the time to do it. The old truth is still true today, 'God helps those who help themselves.' My advice? Meditate."*

Tony Schwartz, CEO of Energy Project, said in his blog, *"Maintaining a steady reservoir of energy – physically, mentally, emotionally and even spiritually – requires refueling it intermittently."*

Those are just a few successful people who do meditations or have a quiet time each morning.

Here's what I, personally, do in the morning. One of the first things I do when I get up is read my Bible. I always do it; one chapter, every morning. This fills my mind with positive thoughts early in the day. This is my precious time with God. After that, I read a page from a Christian book, and then I pray. This is my way of meditating and having a daily devotion. This gives me peace of mind for the rest of the day. I am happier, more positive, calmer, and more relaxed as I start my day, and that continues throughout the day.

As the Bible says in Joshua 1:8 (NASB), *"This book of the law shall not depart from your mouth, but you shall meditate on it day and night, so that you may be careful to do according to all that is written in it; for then you will make your way prosperous, and then you will have success."*

Did you catch that? Yes, it says right in the Bible, *"for then you will **make your way prosperous**, and then **you will have success**."*

So, if you want to be prosperous and successful, meditate on the word of God first thing in the morning. Connect with Him; be with Him. You can do it by reading one chapter every morning. Start with Proverbs; it has exactly 31 chapters, which means you can do it in 31 days. Doing anything for a month will create a habit.

After reading a chapter from the Bible, spend time praying. Turn your worries and concerns over to God. Let your mind, soul, body, and spirit be renewed and refreshed through prayer and scripture reading. This one habit can dramatically change your life, and it's one which I can personally guarantee because it works for me.

So, my friend, have a quiet time every morning. Remember, this is one of the daily habits of successful people. Why not follow it?

## 4. Successful People Motivate Themselves

One of the things I admire about successful people is their ability to motivate themselves. And they know the best time to do this is in the morning.

How do they motivate themselves? By using visualizations or affirmations.

Arnold Schwarzenegger is really a big fan of visualization. Visualization has always been a part of his life, from winning Mr. Universe titles to winning Mr. Olympia titles, from becoming a number-one box office star to becoming a Governor.

He said in an interview, "What you do is *create a vision* of who you want to be, and then live into that picture as if it were already true."

That's his secret: *visualization*. This was also the secret of the late Muhammad Ali, who visualized himself victorious long before his actual fight. It was the key secret of Jim Carrey when he was a struggling young actor picturing himself being the greatest actor in the world. And it's the secret recipe of success for Michael Jordan who always takes the last shot in his mind before he ever takes one in real life. That's the power of visualization.

Another secret is affirmations.

One of my favorite pastors and virtual mentors is Joel Osteen, Senior Pastor of the largest church in America, Lakewood Church.

If you've attended one of the services at Lakewood or watched him on YouTube, you've probably noticed one thing he does before he preaches – he uses affirmations. His affirmation is called "This is my Bible." Here it is:

*"This is my Bible. I am what it says I am. I can do what it says I can do. Today, I will be taught the Word of God. I boldly confess: My mind is alert, my heart is receptive. I will never be the same. Never, never, never. I will never be the same. In Jesus name. Amen."*

That's a kind of prayer, right? A prayer and affirmation.

I also love reading Joel Osteen's books, and some of the great ones are: *Your Best Life Now*; *Becoming a Better You*; *You Can, You Will*; *Break Out*; and *I Declare*. I've personally read all those books, and I could say that they have truly transformed my life for the better. His book, *I Declare* is filled with affirmations that you can declare over your life every day. One example is:

*"I declare that GOD has a great plan for my life. He is directing my steps. And even though I may not always understand how, I know my situation is not a surprise to GOD. He will work out every detail to my advantage. In His perfect timing, everything will turn out right. This is my declaration."*

Those are the two keys – visualizations and affirmations. Use visualizations as part of your daily life. Follow Arnold Schwarzenegger's example for achieving success. Imitate the secrets used by Muhammad Ali to win boxing championships. Copy the plans of Jim Carrey and Michael Jordan to be one of the greatest at what you do. Use visualizations in your life.

In the morning, and even throughout the day, always affirm and declare great things upon your life, just like Joel Osteen. Visualizations and affirmations – those are two of the secrets of successful people.

## 5. Successful People Grow Themselves

This is one of my favorite morning (or daily) habits of successful people – they grow themselves.

You may be asking, "Andrian, what do you mean they grow themselves?"

What I mean is successful people love learning. They grow themselves by reading self-improvement or personal development books; by reading articles, blogs, or something related to their fields; and by listening to motivational or self-improvement audios or videos.

As Jim Rohn once said, *"If you want to have more, you have to become more. For things to change, you have to change. For things to get better, you have to become better. If you improve, everything will improve for you. If you grow, your money will grow; your relationships, your health, your business, and every external effect will mirror that growth in equal correlation."*

That is what I mean by growing: improving yourself to become more.

John Maxwell, the author of many leadership books such as the most popular one *The 21 Irrefutable Laws of Leadership*, once said, *"You will never change your life until you change something you do daily. The secret of your success is found in your daily routine."*

Two of John Maxwell's habits are reading self-improvement books and listening to personal development audios or videos.

Did you know that during Maxwell's childhood, his parents gave him and his siblings an allowance based on how many self-improvement books they read? Yes, their parents helped them invest in their future early on in their childhood. The more self-improvement books they read, the more allowance they received. Isn't that an amazing way to motivate children to read?

This is one of the reasons why John Maxwell is now considered a leadership guru in today's world. The seeds his parents planted early in his childhood have already grown and continue to grow.

That's the power of growing yourself.

Let's see if you can guess what the following successful people have in common.

Anthony Robbins is the highest-paid motivational speaker on any topic. Darren Hardy is the CEO of *Success Magazine.* Denis Waitley is the best-selling author of the audio series "*The Psychology of Winning.*" Brian Tracy is recognized as the top sales training and personal success authority in the world today. John C. Maxwell is known as the world's leadership guru. Les Brown is one of the world's most renowned motivational speakers. Mark Victor Hansen is known as the founder and co-creator of the *Chicken Soup for the Soul* book series.

Maybe you've already guessed it? Yes, they have all "grown" through reading self-improvement books and listening to personal development audios or videos. But there's one thing that you might not know about these people.

These successful people all have one mentor – Jim Rohn.

Yes, Jim Rohn is the mentor of all these mentors. He is recognized as a master personal development trainer. How did he do it? By changing and growing himself every single day.

So again, friend, if you want to be more successful in life, follow the daily habits of successful people, the habits of rich people, and the habits of successful entrepreneurs – grow yourself more.

Let's recap the list of top five morning routines and habits of successful people again:

- Successful People Get Up Early – Opportunity Clock

- Successful People Exercise

- Successful People Have a Quiet Time

- Successful People Motivate Themselves

- Successful People Grow Themselves

This chapter alone has revealed many keys that you can apply in your own life. And, with that, friend, I'd like to challenge you to share these 'morning habits' with your family and friends so that they, too, would learn and benefit from them. I'm confident they will love these morning habits as well. Not only will you have joy and happiness, but they will appreciate you all the more for sharing this wealth of wisdom. Please feel free to use this link, **www.bit.ly/ilovemorninghabits** to share this book with your family and friends on Facebook.

Before I end this chapter, friend, I would like to share with you a fabulous quote from Marcus Aurelius:

*"When you arise in the morning, think of what a precious privilege it is to be alive; to breathe, to think, to enjoy, to love."*

Friend, make every morning precious. And remember: **You** are precious!

# POSITIVE ENERGY POWER #4: MOTIVATION – 4 SIMPLE WAYS TO GET MOTIVATED IN LIFE

Motivation – this is the driving force behind achieving our dreams and goals in life. Everyone wants to know how to get more motivated in life.

In some cases, we want to achieve our dreams instantaneously, as if by magic.

In life, we often look for shortcuts. Sometimes, we don't want to discipline ourselves to do what really makes us happy, which is achieving our goals. That's where motivation comes in.

How to get and stay motivated in life is something I get asked about a lot. And that's what we'll talk about in this chapter – how to be motivated every single day.

So, come along, friend, and join me on this journey called "life." Let's see how we can motivate ourselves every single day. But first, let's start off with an excellent quote by Zig Ziglar:

*"People often say that motivation doesn't last. Well, neither does bathing – that's why we recommend it daily."*

# Here are 4 Simple Ways to Stay Motivated in Life:

## 1. Write, Rewrite, and Read Your Goals Every Day

There's power in writing, rewriting, and reading your goals every day. Brian Tracy, a goal-setting guru, advises us to write and re-write our goals every day. Here's his suggested technique:

*Each day write down your 10 most important goals without referring to your previous list and do this day after day.*

Remarkably, great things will happen when you do this. On the first day, you write your top 10 goals. And on the second day, you again write your top 10 goals, *but without referring* to the goals you wrote on the first day.

You'll notice that your goals will vary slightly from day to day. But, if you do this every day for 30 days you will notice that after 30 days, you'll have a clear vision of your top 10 goals – the things you *really* want. Your mind is now sharper and more focused on these top 10 goals you have written.

Oh, and did I mention there is a rule you need to follow when you are writing your goals? It's the 3 P's rule – present, positive, and personal.

Your subconscious mind is activated by affirmative statements phrased in the *present* tense. Therefore, you need to write down your goals as if you've already achieved them. Instead of saying, "*I will earn $100,000 in the next 12 months,*" you would say, "*I earn $100,000 per year.*"

Your goals also need to be *positive*. Instead of saying, "*I will not smoke anymore,*" or "*I will lose 20 pounds,*" you would instead say, "*I am a non-smoker,*" or, "*I weigh 140 lbs.*" Your command must be positive so that your subconscious mind will focus on that positive direction.

And lastly, make it *personal*. Your goal must be written as an "*I*" statement followed by a verb (action). You are the only person in the universe who can use the word "I" in relation to yourself. When your subconscious mind receives your command in the form of an "I" statement, it begins processing your request immediately to bring that goal to fruition. So, always start your goals with an "I" statement, such as "I own," "I earn," "I drive," or "I weigh," and so on.

Also, to add power and clarity to your daily goals add a deadline and make it specific.

For example, if you want to earn $100,000 per year, then set a deadline like this: "I earn $100,000 per year by December 20##."

Your mind loves deadlines; they challenge you to do something before that specific time ends. So remember to make it specific – so specific that it propels you to achieve your goals faster, ahead of your scheduled deadline.

Those are the 3 P's you need to remember every single day when writing your goals. In order to be motivated, your goals must be present, positive, and personal.

And don't forget, friend, daily motivation comes from writing, rewriting, and reading your goals every single day.

## 2. Watch Motivational Videos

Want to get motivated? Watch motivational videos. This is one of the keys I used when I was reviewing for my board exam a few years ago.

Every day, I needed motivation. There were times when I didn't feel like doing this or that, reading this or that. But in order to keep myself motivated, I went online and watched motivational videos on YouTube.

This was the spark I needed to do something immediately – as in *right now*.

If you want to get motivated right now – as in *now* – I have the perfect video for you. I still watch this video when I want to get motivated. It's the scene from the movie *Facing the Giants.* I guarantee this will make an impact on you. To watch the video, go to YouTube and type the title *"The Death Crawl scene from Facing the Giants"* (uploaded by Toni DiFranco). Make sure you have your volume up to get the full impact of this motivational scene.)

What did you think? Did it motivate you? Yes, that's one of the videos that I always watch when I need instant motivation. But that's not the only one; there are many, many motivational videos you can watch on YouTube.

Take time to watch and get motivated. Then share the videos with your family and friends so they can be motivated, too.

This one technique for getting motivated instantly will give you the right perspective and persistence to go on with your dreams and goals, as well as enthusiasm to move forward and motivation to get you going.

So friend, give yourself a spark every day to accomplish what you want to achieve in life by watching motivational videos.

## 3. Read Motivational and Inspirational Quotes

I love reading quotes from successful people such as athletes, entrepreneurs, speakers, and others.

This gives me instant food for thought, which is encouraging, motivating, and inspiring.

Actually, I have them printed out and placed on the walls of my home; quotes from people such as Anthony Robbins, John Maxwell, T. Harv Eker, Jim Rohn, Brian Tracy, Jack Canfield, and Stephen Covey. Here are a few examples of the quotes I have put on my walls:

*"If you want to move to a new level in your life, you must break through your comfort zone and practice doing things that are not comfortable." - T. Harv Eker*

*"You will never change your life until you change something you do daily. The secret of your success is found in your daily routine." - John C. Maxwell*

*"If you want to have more, you have to become more. For things to change, you have to change. For things to get better, you have to become better. If you improve, everything will improve for you. If you grow, your money will grow; your relationships, your health, your business and every external effect will mirror that growth in equal correlation." - Jim Rohn*

Those are just three of the many quotes I have printed out and hung on my walls. I see them *every single day*.

But, more importantly, I *read* them. And every time I do, it refocuses my mind in a positive direction, uplifts me to move towards the direction of my goals, and motivates me to keep going, so I can achieve my dreams.

I've even found a fantastic app for smartphones that is designed to get you motivated every day. It's called *"Secrets of Success"* by Dale Carnegie. There are tons of motivational and inspirational quotes within the app that you can read every day.

Or you may want to search the Internet for motivational quotes. It's extremely helpful to have something motivational or inspirational to read before starting your day – something to uplift you and motivate you.

This is the most effective way to start your day because it will tune your thoughts toward a better mood, and you will be headed in a positive direction for the rest of the day.

So again, friend, if you want to get motivated, read motivational and inspirational quotes from successful people. Even if you do this for only two or three minutes every morning, it will have a positive impact on your peace of mind, happiness, and attitude for the rest of the day.

## 4. Get Started, Start Moving – *"Just Do It"* Attitude

The truth is if you really want to be motivated, and you don't want procrastination to be a stumbling block, then get started – just start moving!

Yes, you read that right. Just start doing the things you've been putting off. Don't feel like doing it? Do it anyway. Just *start*. Maybe you are tired, or not in the mood? Do it anyway. Afraid to do it? *Just do it!* Feel the fear and do it anyway.

The key here is to *just do it.*

As Zig Ziglar said:

*"Anything worth doing is worth doing poorly--until you can learn to do it well."*

And as G.K. Chesterton once said:

*"If a thing is worth doing, it is worth doing badly."*

If there is something in life about which you are procrastinating, then start small, one bite at a time. Or, if there's something which you're afraid to do, push yourself to do it anyway.

As Alfred Armand Montapert said:

*"Begin, and you are halfway there."*

The keyword here is "begin."

Friend, if you want to get motivated, then start doing it, *slowly at first, if needed,* until you've gotten that "flow" in you.

And after a while, you will realize you are feeling your passion, your blood is starting to flow, your energy is increasing, and your enthusiasm is coming back again.

It's all because you started, you began doing it.

That's the secret: *Just Do It.*

If you still need a little push in life, then I suggest you watch a one-minute video by Shia LaBeaouf. This video will really motivate you. To watch the video on YouTube, type the title: *"Shia LaBeouf 'Just Do It' Motivational Speech (Original Video)"* uploaded by MotivaShian.

Are you shocked? I was, too, the first time I watched it. But did this video wake you up? Did it motivate you? Did it light a spark inside you, and make you feel you need to do something? Yes, this video motivates many people. It reminds people to *"Just Do It"* and never give up.

Let's look at Shia's lines once again:

*Do it!*

*Just do it!*

*Don't let your dreams be dreams.*

*Yesterday you said tomorrow.*

*So just do it!*

*Make your dreams come true!*

*Just do it!*

*Some people dream success, while you're gonna wake up and work hard at it.*

*Nothing is impossible!*

*You should get to the point where anyone else would quit,*

*and you're not gonna stop there!*

*No! What are you waiting for?!*

*Just do it!*

*Just DO it!*

*Yes, you CAN!*

*JUST DO IT!*

*If you're tired of starting over, STOP GIVING UP!*

Wow! What an inspiration! Truly motivational: *Just Do It!*

Did this video motivate you? Yes, I believe it did.

Friend, you only have one life to live. If you want to achieve something in your life, you've got to get started, you've got to do the things that you want to achieve. You've got to do it, *just do it!*

Do It. Do it! Do! It!

*NOW!*

That's the secret – do it **now**.

One of my favorite affirmations which motivates me, comes from chapter 16 of Og Mandino's book, "*The Greatest Salesman in the World.*" (I'm including it below. I recommend that you mark this page, and when you get a moment alone, read it aloud.)

"*I will act now. I will act now. I will act now. Henceforth, I will repeat these words, again and again, each hour, every day, until the words become a habit as my breathing and the actions which follow become as instinctive as the blinking of my eyelids. With these words, I can condition my mind to meet every challenge.*"

So again, friend, if you want to get motivated, then get started; start moving, *"JUST DO IT,"* and "*ACT NOW.*"

There you have it, four simple ways to get motivated in life. As a recap, here they are:

- Write, Rewrite, and Read Your Goals Every Day

- Watch Motivational Videos

- Read Motivational and Inspirational Quotes

- Get Started, Start Moving – "*Just Do It*" Attitude

Before I end this chapter, friend, I would like to share with you an inspirational quote from Anthony Robbins:

*"At any moment, the decision you make can change the course of your life forever."*

Friend, every day you have a decision to make: *"Will I take action today or not?"* Get motivated. Get inspired. Take action. Every day, you always have a choice; *"Choose life."*

# POSITIVE ENERGY POWER #5: PRAYER – WHAT IS THE POWER OF PRAYER? SIX TIPS ON HOW TO PLUG INTO THE POWER OF PRAYER

This year, have you been asking God for something amazing to happen in your life? Have you been praying for your goals? Have you already reached them?

In this chapter, we're going to answer the following questions about prayer: What is the power of prayer? Is praying really effective? How do I plug into the power of prayer? Is there abundance in prayer? Is there really *power in prayer*?

These are questions many people ask when it comes to the topic of prayer. If you want to achieve great things in your life and want to have a happy, positive, and peaceful life, you have to know and utilize the *amazing* power of prayer.

## What is the Power of Prayer?

The power of prayer is **the power of GOD**, who hears and answers our prayers.

Praying is an act of communicating with God. You probably already talk to God, in your own way. Guess what? That means you're praying!

Most people pray for:

provisions, healings, abundance, good health, goals and dreams, forgiveness, restoration, family, protection, strength, wisdom, relationship, money, and anything else we want to achieve in life.

Sometimes we receive these things we pray for quickly, but often we don't.

In this chapter, we will discover: how to tap into this amazing power of prayer; how God answers prayers; and what are the things we need to do for God to answer our prayers.

Are you ready?

Okay, friend, sit back and relax. We're about to learn how to tap into the amazing power of prayer.

# The 6 Tips for Plugging Into the Power of Prayer:

## 1. Your Prayer Must Be According to God's Will

In I John 5:14-15, the Bible says, *"This is the confidence we have in approaching God: that if we ask anything according to His will, He hears us. And if we know that He hears us—whatever we ask—we know that we have what we asked of Him."*

Yes, our prayer must be according to God's will. But some of you may ask, "Andrian, how do I know God's will for my life?"

According to Chris Russell, there are eight keys to knowing God's will in our lives:

### a. Walk with God

You will never know God's will for your life if you're not walking with Him. Walking with God means you need to know Him deeply, have a relationship with Him, communicate with Him through prayer, and listen as God communicates with you through His Word.

### b. Surrender Your Will to God

Whatever plans you have, always remember God is still the one Who decides what's best for you. So, surrender your plans to God. Proverbs 20:24 tells us *"a man's steps are directed by the LORD."* You plan, but let God direct your steps.

## c. Obey What You Already Know to be God's Will

You already know that jeopardizing your health (e.g., smoking and drinking) is not God's will for your life. You need to stop those bad habits. It says in Jeremiah 29:11, *"'For I know the plans I have for you,' declares the Lord, 'plans to prosper you and not to harm you, plans to give you hope and a future.'"* Do not harm yourself by doing things that you know are not healthy for you. God's plans for you are always for your wellbeing.

## d. Seek Godly Input

Hang out with other Christians. By being with them, you can ask for advice and learn their ways. It's better to be around real Christians than to be around those who will influence you negatively. Proverbs 15:22 says, *"Plans fail for lack of counsel, but with many advisers they succeed."* So choose your advisers wisely. Seek Godly input.

## e. Pay Attention to How God Has Wired You

You are gifted at something. You are excellent at something. God has given you talents and abilities because He wants you to use them for His glory. In 1 Peter 4:10 (NKJV), it states, *"As each one has received a gift, minister it to one another, as good stewards of the manifold grace of God."* You have a talent, a gift, an ability – use it! Because that's what God's will is for your life.

## f. Listen to God's Spirit

In your prayer time, don't just talk to God, take time to listen, as well. Listen to what God is saying. He will reveal great things to you when you take the time to listen. In John 10:27, it states, "*My sheep hear My voice, and I know them, and they follow Me.*" Take time to listen to God, and He will reveal to you the next steps you need to take.

## g. Listen to Your Heart

Yes, in addition to listening to God's Spirit, you must also listen to your heart.

In Psalm 37:4-5 (NKJV) it states:

"*Delight yourself also in the LORD, and He shall give you the desires of your heart. Commit your way to the LORD, trust also in Him, and he shall bring it to pass.*"

God has given us the desires of our hearts for a reason. And we have different desires. My desires may be different from yours, and your desires may be different from mine.

If you want to know God's will for your life, then listen to what your heart is telling you. God created our hearts to discern things which God wants us to do or not do. It's sort of like signals, or warnings, about whether what we are about to do is God's best for us or not.

As the old adage says, "Follow your heart."

## h. Take a Look at Your Circumstances

There's always a reason why things are happening in your life. Often, things happen because God wants to get your attention. You may not know it, but God is already working out His plans for your life.

Always be alert on what's happening around you; see where God is taking you, notice your circumstances and make it work to your advantage. Because God is already working things out for your own good.

In Acts 16:6-10 (NKJV) we see an illustration of God's plans for Paul and his entourage:

*"Now when they had gone through Phrygia and the region of Galatia, they were forbidden by the Holy Spirit to preach the word in Asia. After they had come to Mysia, they tried to go into Bithynia, but the Spirit did not permit them. So passing by Mysia, they came down to Troas. And a vision appeared to Paul in the night. A man of Macedonia stood and pleaded with him, saying, 'Come over to Macedonia and help us.' Now after he had seen the vision, immediately we sought to go to Macedonia, concluding that the Lord had called us to preach the gospel to them."*

Take a look at your circumstances. How is God directing you toward His great plans for your life?

There you have it: eight keys to knowing God's will for your life.

## 2. Your Prayer Must Be Consistent and Persistent

The Bible tells us to *"pray without ceasing"* in 1 Thessalonians 5:17. That means we are to continue praying, to continue seeking God's direction for our lives.

Now, let's look at Matthew 7:7-8 and see how it elaborates (ask, seek, knock) on this concept:

*"Ask and it will be given to you; seek and you will find; knock and the door will be opened to you. For everyone who asks receives; the one who seeks finds; and to the one who knocks, the door will be opened."*

The first stage is **asking** – the word to remember is **"petition."** We must pray by asking of God first, by petitioning Him for what we want.

Then, the second stage is **seeking** – the word to remember here is **"participation."** We must pray by asking, but we also need to do something. We need to take action on what we are praying for. It requires our participation.

Finally, the third stage is **knocking** - the word to remember here is **"persistence."** We have asked, and we have taken action, but now we need to continually do it over and over again until God answers – that's persistence.

This is what God is implying when he tells us to pray without ceasing: petition, participation, and persistence.

So, friend, always pray, pray and pray some more. That's the secret. Persistence is one of the keys to God answering your prayer.

## 3. Your Prayer Must Be With Thanksgiving

The Bible states in Philippians 4:6, *"Do not be anxious about anything, but in every situation, by prayer and petition, with thanksgiving, present your requests to God."*

This is a very powerful principle in praying. Before you can have what you're praying for, you need to begin thanking God ahead of time. Start praising Him, thanking Him, as if it has already happened. Your gratitude, praise, and thanksgiving open doors that only God can open.

Let's look at the power of thanksgiving and praising God ahead of time by learning about Paul and Silas from Acts 16:23-26. I'm going to paraphrase, but you'll get the idea.

Both men were severely beaten and put into prison. The jailer was told to watch them carefully, so he placed their feet in shackles.

Around midnight, Paul and Silas were **praying and singing hymns to God**. You can imagine how this caught the attention of the other prisoners.

All of a sudden there was a strong earthquake that shook the very foundations of the prison. Then all the doors swung open, and everyone's chains fell off.

Yes, that actually happened. That's the power of thanksgiving, gratitude, and praise to God. He can shake foundations and open doors for you that no man can shut.

In Psalm 100:4 (NKJV), the Bible states, *"Enter into His gates with thanksgiving, and into His courts with praise: be thankful to Him, and bless His name."*

As you pray, give thanks to God as if He has already answered you. Praise Him, sing hymns to Him, bless His name, and thank Him in advance. Be grateful and have an attitude of gratitude ahead of time. You will see the miraculous power of God as He opens doors for you that no man can shut.

I have another video for you to watch. It is Terri Savelle Foy speaking on the power of gratitude, thanksgiving, and praising God *before* God opens doors of blessings and opportunities in our lives. To watch the video on YouTube, search for the title, *"The Power of Gratitude"* uploaded by Terri Savelle Foy. This video will help you understand how God's blessings continually come into your life through the power of thanksgiving.

I believe you will learn a lot from this video. It shows how powerful our prayer is when we give thanks to the Lord ahead of time.

So, friend, pray with thanksgiving and you will see doors of blessings and opportunities open that no man can shut.

## 4. Your Prayer Must Give Glory to God

The Bible states in John 14:13-14, *"And I will do whatever you ask in My name, so that the Father may be glorified in the Son. You may ask Me for anything in My name, and I will do it."*

Jesus wants us to pray in His name so that God will be glorified. You can ask God for anything that will glorify Him, and He will surely do it for you.

In John 17:4 (NASB), Jesus said, *"I glorified You on the earth, having accomplished the work which You have given Me to do."*

We glorify God by doing the work He gives us.

You have a passion, I have a passion – we all know we have a passion for something. There is a little voice in our head that tells us we can do *that something* better than anyone else.

Glorify God by doing those things which you're passionate about. God wired you specifically for that passion because He wants to use you for His glory.

The 2015 NBA MVP, Stephen Curry, the star of the crowned 2015 NBA Champion Golden State Warriors, is a Christian. It is his desire that while he's playing basketball that people will notice something different about him. He plays the game – his passion – for the glory of God.

When God is glorified by what you do, He will be pleased and give you more blessings in life.

Joel Osteen, the senior pastor of the largest church in America, Lakewood Church, is passionate about giving *hope* to people. His dad, John Osteen, loves sharing about the *power of the Holy Spirit.* John C. Maxwell, a teaching pastor at Christ Fellowship, is passionate about sharing *leadership* skills with people. Joyce Meyer's passion is the *power of thoughts.* And Terri Savelle Foy is passionate about sharing *how to achieve dreams and goals.*

Note: Although these ministries seem similar, they are each different. And, they are each glorifying God through the passions He gave them, through what He assigned for them to do here on earth. That's why they have received so many blessings from the Lord.

So, what's your passion? What do you do, that when you do it, God is glorified? Maybe your passion is swimming, or painting, or architecture, or graphic design or mountain climbing. Whatever it is, give glory to God when you do it, and God will give you more than you can ask for or imagine.

The Bible states in Colossians 3:17, *"And whatever you do, whether in word or deed, do it all in the name of the Lord Jesus, giving thanks to God the Father through Him."*

So, friend, give God the glory, and you will receive the overflowing blessings that God has in store for you.

## 5. Your Prayer Must Come With a Humble and Sincere Heart

The Bible states in 2 Chronicles 34:27:

*"Because your heart was responsive and you humbled yourself before God when you heard what he spoke against this place and its people, and because you humbled yourself before Me and tore your robes and wept in My presence, I have heard you, declares the Lord."*

Do you want your prayer to be heard by God? Then, come before Him with a humble and sincere heart.

A fabulous illustration of how God answers the man who has a humble and sincere heart when praying can be found in Luke 18:10-14 below. This passage talks about the prayers of the Pharisee and tax collector, two very different men.

*"Two men went up to the temple to pray, one a Pharisee and the other a tax collector. The Pharisee stood by himself and prayed: 'God, I thank you that I am not like other people—robbers, evildoers, adulterers—or even like this tax collector. I fast twice a week and give a tenth of all I get.'*

*"But the tax collector stood at a distance. He would not even look up to heaven, but beat his breast and said, 'God, have mercy on me, a sinner.'*

*"I tell you that this man, rather than the other, went home justified before God. For all those who exalt themselves will be humbled, and those who humble themselves will be exalted."*

In this story, we learn that when we humble ourselves before God, He exalts us. Like us, the tax collector was a sinner; yet he humbled himself before God, and God heard his prayer and justified him.

Truly, God blesses the people who pray with a humble and sincere heart.

So again, friend, if you want God to answer your prayers, have a humble and sincere heart. God will bless you more than what you can even ask or imagine.

## 6. Your Prayer Must Be Filled With Faith

The Bible says in James 1:5-7,

*"If any of you lacks wisdom, you should ask God, who gives generously to all without finding fault, and it will be given to you. But when you ask, you must believe and not doubt, because the one who doubts is like a wave of the sea, blown and tossed by the wind. That person should not expect to receive anything from the Lord."*

Pray in Faith – that's our last lesson here on how to tap into the power of prayer and receive answers from God. You must believe and not doubt when you pray. You must believe that God can do anything for you, no matter what it may be, whether big or small.

Have you been praying to God for something and God hasn't answered your prayer yet? Maybe God sees doubt in your heart. Believe in God *fully and completely*, that He can do this for you. God can handle anything for you once you *believe*.

The Bible says in Matthew 21:22, *"If you believe, you will receive whatever you ask for in prayer."*

The key here is to believe.

Once God sees in your heart that you really believe and that you have sought His will for your life, He will do whatever you ask. Whatever you're praying for – a new house, a new car, a vacation you've been dreaming about – God can give it to you when you **believe.**

Also, pray for God-sized prayers, pray bold prayers, pray for big things from God. God is a *big* GOD, the creator of the universe. He can give you whatever you ask for; just believe in Him.

So again, friend, have faith in God that He will answer your prayers, and He will do miracles for you that you have never experienced before.

So there it is. We have answered the questions, "What is the power of prayer?" and "How do I plug into the power of prayer?" Just to recap, here are the six keys to remember for God to answer your prayer:

- Your Prayer Must Be According To God's Will

- Your Prayer Must Be Consistent and Persistent

- Your Prayer Must Be With Thanksgiving

- Your Prayer Must Give Glory To God

- Your Prayer Must Come With A Humble And Sincere Heart

- Your Prayer Must Be Filled With Faith

These six tips on prayer will build your faith and enable you to tap into the power of God, who is able to do immeasurably more than what you can ask or imagine.

And before I end this chapter, friend, I want to share with you a beautiful quote from A.P.J. Abdul Kalam:

*"God, our Creator, has stored within our minds and personalities, great potential strength and ability. Prayer helps us tap and develop these powers."*

Friend, the power of prayer is already within you. Tap into it, plug into it, and develop that true power within you.

# POSITIVE ENERGY POWER #6: FORGIVENESS – LIFE POWER PRINCIPLE: WHAT IS THE POWER OF FORGIVENESS?

Boomerang.

This is a curved stick which, when thrown in a certain way, will come back to you.

Have you already seen a boomerang? Or have you already seen someone who throws a boomerang, and it *magically* comes back to him? It is like magic, isn't it? Well, if you have never seen it, here's a video I found on YouTube showing how a boomerang really goes back to the one who throws it. To watch the video on YouTube, search for the title: "*How to throw a 'traditional shaped returning' boomerang"* uploaded by Victor Poulin.

Did you watch it? Did you see how the boomerang returns to the man who throws it? It's amazing, right?

When I see this video, I am simply amazed because I really don't know how boomerangs work. But then I realize the power of a boomerang; it's awesome!

Now, some of you are probably confused and asking, "Andrian, I thought this chapter was about forgiveness. Why are you showing us this boomerang thing?"

Well, yes, friend, I want to tell you that forgiveness and unforgiveness are like that – it's like a boomerang.

When you have unforgiveness in your heart and hatred towards someone who has hurt you, the effect of these feelings can come back to you. It could be in the form of illness, disease, uncomfortableness, sleepless nights, inefficiency, lack of decision, and so on.

In short, you are blocking blessings, happiness, joy, peace, abundance, and freedom from coming into your life.

Karen Swartz, M.D., Associate Professor of Psychiatry and Behavioral Sciences at Johns Hopkins

Hospital, confirms that "*there is an enormous physical burden to being hurt and disappointed.*"

When you are always angry, your body reacts physically by being ready to either fight or flee. This causes changes in your blood pressure and your body's immunities.

Think about the last time you were angry. How did you feel afterwards? Chances are, you didn't feel so good.

But, when we forgive, our stress levels are calmed, and our health improves.

Studies done at Stanford University have shown that anger adds stress to our lives and affects our cardiovascular system.

Studies have shown that you can improve your physical health – even after a heart attack – by practicing forgiveness. It's not always easy; sometimes you need to work at it to be more tolerant and let go of the anger inside of you.

But, when you learn how to forgive, you will see that all blessings will naturally come back to you: the good physical health, the happiness, the love, the joy, the peace, the freedom, the abundance, and many blessings of life. Yes, just like a boomerang, they will return to you the moment you forgive.

That's the powerful principle of forgiveness.

As I said, forgiveness isn't always easy, and it can lead to many questions, such as: "How do I forgive someone who has hurt me?" "How do I forgive friends?" "How do I forgive myself for past mistakes?" "What is the power of forgiveness, and how can it change my life?"

These are the questions we will answer in this chapter. You will be amazed at how your life will definitely change once you learn about the healing power of forgiveness.

Are you ready?

Sit back, relax, and enjoy reading – because now we're going to learn the answers to these questions which we so often ask about forgiveness.

## What is the Power of Forgiveness?

The Bible says in Isaiah 1:18 (NKJV), *"'Come now, and let us reason together,' says the LORD, 'though your sins are like scarlet, they shall be as white as snow; though they are red like crimson, they shall be as wool.'"*

Forgiveness cleanses you from the baggage you have been carrying around. It washes you, and you become white as snow, clearing your mind, cleansing your soul and spirit, and healing your body. That's the power of forgiveness.

We can't really understand the power of forgiveness until we know the Best Forgiver of all – our Almighty God.

God forgives at all times.

God's grace and mercy are always around us. His amazing love for us is overflowing. If we want to know the power of forgiveness, first we need to receive God's love, mercy, and grace. But how can we do that?

The Bible says in 1 John 1:9 (NKJV), *"If we confess our sins, He is faithful and just to forgive us our sins, and to cleanse us from all unrighteousness."*

Confessing our sins to God allows us to release this guilt and condemnation we have hidden inside of us.

And God will cleanse us from all this bondage and unrighteousness. God is always willing to forgive us no matter what we've done. He is always willing to accept us.

Later, I will show you how to pray for forgiveness from God, and how to forgive ourselves.

## How Do You Forgive Yourself for Past Mistakes?

Most of the time, when we find it hard to forgive others, it's because we haven't forgiven ourselves yet for similar things we've done.

The past mistakes, the sins, are weighing us down and making us feel guilty and condemned.

This is why we aren't able to forgive others either. As someone once said, *"You cannot give what you don't have."*

But once we fathom and receive the forgiveness of God in our lives, we will realize how easy it is to forgive others.

The Bible states in 1 John 3:21 (NASB), *"Beloved, if our heart does not condemn us, we have confidence before God."*

Friend, always remember this: *Forgiveness starts within you.*

If you want to receive God's forgiveness and love, and at the same time you want to forgive yourself for past mistakes, you may pray this simple prayer:

*"God, I know I am a sinner. I've done some terrible things, and I've done sinful things. But, today I want to confess all my sins to You (go ahead and tell God all of your sins). And, God, I ask You to forgive me from all of my sins. Forgive me, LORD. In Jesus' name, Amen."*

After praying that prayer, accept the love and forgiveness of God through faith, and pray this prayer:

*"LORD, today I accept your forgiveness through faith. I know I am now forgiven by You. You have cleansed me as white as snow according to Your Word. May Your love always be upon me, and may I show others Your love and forgiveness by sharing it with them. Thank You, LORD. I am now releasing the condemnation and guilt. I'm now cutting them out of my life. I am now free. I am now free. In Jesus' name, Amen."*

If you pray that prayer, you will receive God's peace and joy in your heart, and He will allow His blessings to come upon you as you trust in Him and receive His love and forgiveness in your life.

You are now free. Yes, friend, you are now free.

Let me be the first to congratulate you, friend, for the freedom that you have just received. High five!

Now, since you have forgiven yourself and received God's love and forgiveness in your life, I believe you are ready for the next section, and that is...

## How Do You Forgive Someone Who Has Hurt You?

As the Bible says in Colossians 3:13, *"Bear with each other and forgive one another if any of you has a grievance against someone. Forgive as the Lord forgave you."*

In the New Living Translation, the same verse says, *"Make allowance for each other's faults, and forgive anyone who offends you. Remember, the Lord forgave you, so you must forgive others."*

Notice, friend, it says, *"Remember, the LORD forgave you."* Yes, past tense! You have *already* been forgiven by the LORD, and the LORD wants you to forgive others as well.

Someone may have offended you for some reason. You may have been abused or deceived by someone.

You may have been hurt by extended family members, siblings, or friends.

You may have been offended by things said to you by coworkers or somebody close in your life. Whoever it was, you have been hurt.

But remember what we just read – the Bible advises us to "*make allowance for each other's faults.*"

The Bible teaches us in Luke 6:27-28, to "*Love your enemies, do good to those who hate you, bless those who curse you, pray for those who mistreat you.*"

Some of you may be thinking, "But, Andrian, it's very hard. You don't know what happened. It's really hard to forgive that person, you know?"

Yes, I know it's hard. Yes, I know it's difficult. But let's try it anyway.

Have you ever tried blessing someone who has hurt you? Have you tried praying for him/her in your mind? Maybe you haven't tried it yet, but I did. And something miraculous happened. It changed me. The peace flowed through my body, and I felt the relief, the joy, and the freedom of God's love.

Did you know that once you've done what the LORD is asking you to do – this thing that is hard for you to do – you will see the consequences in your life? Yes, right after you pray and bless someone who has hurt you, you will feel peace inside. Try it. Then you will know and understand what I'm talking about.

Tom Holladay, a teaching pastor at Saddleback Church in Lake Forest, CA, beautifully puts it this way:

*"How do you pray for somebody who has hurt you? King David, a man after God's own heart, prayed for people who insulted and rejected him. You can find many of those prayers in the book of Psalms. What I love about his prayers is that he begins many of them by telling God his honest feelings about the people who hurt him.*

*"That's how our prayers should start.*

*"Don't pretend to be pious; God knows what is on your mind anyway. Tell God how you honestly feel. Admit you are struggling to pray for the other person, but then ask God to bless him or her.*

*"Honest and humble prayers have the power to make a difference in this world."*

God wants you to release anything negative you harbor in your heart towards someone else – give it to Him. That's why God wants you to forgive others who have hurt you; He wants you to be free from their chains, to take away their power over you.

He wants you to have freedom. He wants you to receive more blessings in your life.

Because when you do not forgive someone – or you have a grudge or resentment toward someone – you are blocking the blessings of God and preventing them from coming into your life.

That's why it's very important to forgive quickly, as the Bible says in Colossians 3:13 (MSG), *"Forgive as quickly and completely as the Master forgave you."*

So the moment someone hurts you, *forgive immediately*. Let it go. That's very important, to forgive quickly, so it will not return to your mind over and over again. This will give you more peace and freedom.

Also, did you know you are consuming a lot of energy when you are angry? It consumes your time when you are thinking about someone or something that has offended you.

As Joyce Meyer said, *"I have learned that any day I spend angry and offended is a wasted day. Life is too short and too precious to waste any of it."*

## When someone offends you, ask yourself...

*"Will I let him/her control my mind, my time, my energy? My life is too precious to be consumed by this. I would rather choose to be happy and enjoy my life. I am willing to forgive him/her."*

Then do this technique which I personally use. Go to a place where you can be alone, close your eyes, and do this:

*Think of the person who offended you. Imagine that he/she is in front of you right now. Talk to him/her like you're talking to him/her personally. Tell him/ her, "You know what, (Name), I have been offended by what you've done or said (be specific on what he/she has done or said), but maybe you've done/said that because you have a reason (think objectively why he/she did or said that – in a positive perspective). But now, I want to forgive you. I'm willing to forgive you. I want to release you right now. Please forgive me if there's anything I have done or said toward you. I'm sorry. But today, right now, I'm choosing to forgive you. I'm forgiving you and releasing you. And today I am now free. I'm now free." In Jesus' name, Amen.' Next, imagine you are releasing him/her from your life.*

## Peace – Serenity – Love – Joy

These are the things you will feel after you've done that exercise. Isn't it so comforting? Isn't it so relieving?

Yes, it is. And that's the power of forgiveness. You can repeat that to every person that might have hurt you in the past, even if it happened many years ago. You will feel peace inside of you, and you will be able to say, "Yes... whew! What a relief! Yes, I can forgive. Yeah. I am now free. I am now free."

Remember, friend, "Forgiveness starts within you."

It's all in your *mind*.

You can forgive anytime you want. You can be free anytime you want.

The techniques above can be done with any relationship you have or have had in the past. You can now forgive friends, family members, or anyone else who has hurt you.

Friend, always remember, that God loves you.

God wants to give you peace, love, joy, happiness, abundance, prosperity, and many other blessings upon your life.

Practice forgiveness in your daily living, and you will receive the abundant blessings God has in store for you.

Once again my friend, if you love this chapter about forgiveness, please share it with your family and friends so they may learn about forgiveness as well. Here is an easy link for you to share this book with your family and friends on Facebook: **www.bit.ly/iloveforgiveness**

Before I end this chapter, I would like to share with you a very beautiful quote by Mahatma Gandhi:

*"The weak can never forgive. Forgiveness is the attribute of the strong."*

Friend, always remember that you are strong because you forgive.

# POSITIVE ENERGY POWER #7: GRATITUDE – WHAT IS AN ATTITUDE OF GRATITUDE? AND THE 3 BENEFITS OF THIS TO YOUR LIFE

I have heard many people ask the following questions:

"What is an attitude of gratitude?"

"Can an attitude of gratitude change my life?"

"What are the benefits of having an attitude of gratitude?"

How often in life do you catch yourself complaining? Or how often do you find yourself seeing the negative things in life more than the positive? Or, to put it plainly, do you have more bad hair days than good ones?

Hmm. If you answered yes to that last question, it's okay, friend. But you know what? Maybe you're missing out on something very essential in your life, something that when applied and developed it can drastically change your life.

Yes, I assure you, it will change the way you think and your perspective on life; it will give you more enthusiasm and happiness in life.

Here is the secret: An attitude of gratitude.

Yes, this simple thought adjustment can dramatically change your life.

Let's start by answering the question, "What is an attitude of gratitude?"

For me, it is simply seeing beauty and being thankful for everything in your life *right now*.

It's about being grateful for everything, even the little things, right now.

It may be for the food you have in your refrigerator, the computer you use to connect to the Internet, or even the shampoo and soap you use in the shower.

An attitude of gratitude sees even the smallest thing, the smallest act, the smallest service, and is always thankful for all of it.

"*Thank you's*" can be used everywhere. A quick "*thank you*" to the person who serves you in a restaurant, or saying "*thank you*" to the bus driver who drives you to work, can really make a big impact not just on your day, but also on the day of those whom you have thanked so genuinely.

That's an attitude of gratitude.

And in this chapter, I'm going to walk you through the benefits of having an attitude of gratitude in your life.

# Here are the 3 Benefits of Having an Attitude of Gratitude in Your Life:

## 1. Gratitude Can Make You Happy Instantly

Yes, instantly! Do you want a proof?

Okay, let's do an experiment. Go get a pen and a piece of paper; list 10 things that you are grateful for right now. You can write *anything*, and I do mean *anything*, which you can think about.

Go, now! Stop reading. I'll wait.

Well, did you do it? What did you feel? Or should I say, "How do you feel now?" Do you feel happy now? See! I told you so!

Maybe you couldn't stop writing after the 10th thing. Maybe you surpassed that and wrote 12, 15, or more than 20 things on your gratitude list. That's okay;

notice the wonderful effect of an attitude of gratitude in your life.

Isn't that a great feeling? What if you did this every day? What if you did this 365 days of the year? You can imagine the cumulative effect that this will have in your life. You'll be happier, calmer, and feel a deeper sense of purpose. You will be more positive than ever before.

That's the power of gratitude.

As William Arthur Ward puts it, "*Gratitude can transform common days into thanksgivings, turn routine jobs into joy, and change ordinary opportunities into blessings.*"

So, friend, always be grateful for everything you have. The more you say "*thank you,*" the happier you will be.

## 2. Gratitude Can Make You Healthier

It's true, an attitude of gratitude can make you healthier. Many studies have proven this to be a fact.

Here's the proof: There was one study conducted by Robert A. Emmons, Ph.D. (University of California), and Mike McCullough (University of Miami), wherein participants were . divided into three groups.

Each group was given a different task. The first group was assigned to keep a journal of those things that they were grateful for in the past week.

The second group was assigned to keep the exact opposite type of journal from the first group. In other words, they were to specifically note the hassles they had in the past week.

The third group was assigned to keep a journal on what affected them in the past week whether it was positive or negative.

Care to guess what the results were?

After 10 weeks of journaling, members of the group that kept the gratitude journals were feeling a lot better about their lives as a whole and were 25% happier than those who kept a journal focusing on the hassles in their lives.

The study also confirmed that those in the gratitude group reported fewer health complaints, and exercised an average of 1.5 hours more.

That is amazing, isn't it? That's how powerful gratitude is – but it doesn't end there.

A later study by Emmons used those same participants, but this time, instead of completing their gratitude journal every week, they were assigned to keep their gratitude journals *daily*.

What was the final outcome of this experiment?

Those participants in the gratitude group became more sympathetic toward others.

They are now kinder, offer others emotional support, and help others with personal problems.

Not only can we reap these benefits of gratitude in our lives, but many studies have also shown that being grateful can improve our sleep habits by allowing us more rest each night, which makes us feel more refreshed each morning.

Also, those who keep gratitude journals *every day* feel more satisfaction with life as a whole, more positive and optimistic about the coming week, and more connected with others in a whole new way.

So, keep a gratitude journal daily. The best time to do this is in the morning so that your thoughts will be moving in the direction of positivity and gratefulness each day.

Always remember, friend, "*When you start the day right, your whole day will be bright.*" Start your day with gratitude, and you will see the positive effects for the rest of your day.

## 3. Gratitude Attracts the Things You Want and Desire

Yes, once again we see the law of attraction.

Have you ever noticed how the law of attraction manifests itself in your life? Have you ever used this law before? Are you aware that you are already using it in your life?

Allow me to answer for you: Yes. The law of attraction manifests itself depending on the thoughts you are sending into the universe, those vibrations which you send, either positive or negative.

The result? It's also either positive or negative.

Did you know that when you're thankful and grateful for everything you have, you are sending positive vibrations to the universe, and you are telling it that you are prepared to receive more into your life?

The law of attraction manifests itself in me a lot of times. It is those times which I'm really thankful for everything God has given me, even the smallest things. That's why God has blessed me so much in my life.

One technique I've been using is the power of prayer which we talked about in the previous chapter.

Every morning, I spend time with God; I read my Bible, pray, and worship Him. It is during that time I praise God and thank Him for all the things He has done for me, and I thank Him for all the desires of my heart which I know He will give me.

And it seems like miracles continually come to me every single day. I am amazed by all the great things God has done for me. I know it is because I've chosen to have an attitude of gratitude, because I am thankful for everything I have – that is why God has blessed me so much.

Yet, I know, some of you are asking, "Andrian, what's the connection between the law of attraction and being thankful and praising God?"

I will tell you: The law of attraction can be found in the Bible.

In Proverbs 23:7 (NKJV), it says, *"As [a man] thinks in his heart, so is he."*

Meaning, whatever you think about, you will attract, and you will become.

If you think about all the good things in your life, you will attract good things.

At the same time, if you think about all the blessings you now have, and if you will be thankful for them, you will attract more of them.

That's the law of attraction, and that's the law of God, as well, according to the Bible.

Allow me to share here the things which I personally do to attract blessings into my life:

a) **Pray** – Always pray for everything you want. If it's God's will, He will grant it. But you need to be patient because God's timing is always perfect.

b) **Praise** – Praising God and thanking Him in advance for all the desires of your heart will attract more of those positive blessings which you want in your life, just like a magnet. Always praise and thank God in advance.

c) **Positive Self-talk** – Wherever you are, you are always talking to yourself through your thoughts. So remember to always say things which boost your confidence, motivate you, and energize you, like *"You are beautiful/handsome." "You are awesome." "Great job, you've nailed it!"*

d) **Be with Positive People** – I always encourage everyone to be around positive people; those who help you, nurture you, guide you, and support you. Stay close to positive people. You can find them in church, or in a club related to your hobbies or passion, or in an online community that is designed to encourage and motivate you.

Always remember, friend, to be grateful for everything you have, and always be positive. You'll notice that you attract more of what you want when you keep your mind focused on an attitude of gratitude.

Those are the top three benefits of an attitude of gratitude. Here's a quick recap of those benefits:

1. Gratitude can make you happy instantly

2. Gratitude can make you healthier

3. Gratitude attracts the things which you want and desire

There you go, friend. We've just answered the questions, "What is an attitude of gratitude?" and "What are the benefits of gratitude in our lives?"

I know I've given you a lot to think over regarding these insights about the benefits of gratitude.

Friend, before I end this chapter, I would like to share with you two outstanding quotes from Philip Yancey and John Milton:

*"What I see in the Bible, especially in the book of Psalms, which is a book of gratitude for the created world, is a recognition that all good things on Earth are God's, every good gift is from above. They are good if we recognize where they came from and if we treat them the way the Designer intended them to be treated." (Philip Yancey)*

*"Gratitude bestows reverence, allowing us to encounter everyday epiphanies, those transcendent moments of awe that change forever how we experience life and the world." (John Milton)*

Friend, always have an attitude of gratitude and life will reveal new and amazing blessings for you.

# POSITIVE ENERGY POWER #8: SUCCESS – 11 CHARACTERISTICS OF HIGHLY SUCCESSFUL PEOPLE

I always love to study and learn about the characteristics of highly successful people. Do they really have common characteristics that have helped them attain success in life? Do they really have qualities which, if I emulate them, will also put me at the peak of success? Friend, have you also asked the question, "What are the characteristics of highly successful people?"

Well today, I'm going to give you the keys, qualities, and characteristics of highly successful people.

But before we start, let me share with you a quote from Darren Hardy, the publisher and founding editor of Success Magazine:

*"Everything you need to be great is already inside you. Stop waiting for someone or something to light your fire. You have the match."*

You read that right, friend. Everything that is needed to be successful is already inside of you. So let's unleash the power that's already inside of you.

# Here are 11 Characteristics of Highly Successful People:

### 1. Focus

Highly successful people know how to focus. They have this kind of laser-targeted focus that helps them achieve what they really want. They know what they need to do. They know what has to be done. They know how to prioritize. And most of the time, they know when to say "No."

As Larry Page, co-founder of Google, says, *"You should focus on one important goal, and you need to be pretty single-minded about it."*

It's challenging to finish a task without a single-minded focus. Try to do 3 different things at once, and you'll discover it's tough to get anything done. However, once you make up your mind and focus on one thing at a time, you will find yourself becoming more efficient than ever before.

So focus, friend. Because "You are a highly successful person."

## 2. 'Push Yourself Out Of Your Comfort Zone' Attitude

One of the things I like most about successful people is the fact that they are all "expanded." You're probably asking, "Andrian, what do you mean by expanded?" When I say expanded, I mean that they have grown a lot and expanded their comfort zone as much as they can.

They don't settle for little things. If they have already mastered something, or have already been comfortable on one level, they will move immediately to the next level – to stretch and expand their comfort zone.

As T. Harv Eker says, *"If you want to move to a new level in your life, you must break through your comfort zone and practice doing things that are not comfortable."*

This is exactly true. If you're experiencing discomfort now, if you're uncomfortable because of the new tasks or new journey which you're going through, that's okay, friend. Why? Because it means you are growing. It means you are expanding. The more you expand, the more you will have.

Push yourself out of your comfort zone, friend, because "You are a highly successful person."

## 3. Persistence

Have you ever found a successful person who failed, or who made some mistakes? Have you ever found a successful person who went through difficult times before they achieved their success? Have you ever found a successful person who really did encounter storms in their life?

Yes, all of the successful people out there today – and I do mean "all" -- are persistent. They might fall down, but they always get back up. They might encounter storms, but they always persevere. They might fail, but they always stand again. They might encounter rejection, but they always lift their head up high and say, "Next."

As Helen Keller says, *"We can do anything we want as long as we stick to it long enough."*

Are you having difficulties right now? Do you think that you've already suffered, that enough is enough, and that you really want to give up on your dreams?

Whatever you may be going through right now, STAY STRONG. You may feel you've already given all you've got, that you've already consumed all the resources you have, but don't forget you may just be "three feet from gold."

So stay strong, friend. Be persistent, because "You are a highly successful person."

## 4. Goal-Oriented

GOAL – do you have a goal? Do you have one target objective this month? Have you written it down? Do you keep it with you?

Did you know that a study done on Harvard MBA Students shows that 3% of the students who wrote down their goals were 10 times more successful (in terms of money made) than 97% of their peers who didn't write down their goals?

Yes, that's how powerful a *written* goal is. Now, let me ask you again: Do you have a written goal? Write it down now and be part of the 3%!

Be goal-oriented, friend, because "You are a highly successful person."

## 5. Action-Taker

Did you know all of the successful people around you are action-takers? Yes, successful people take action. In fact, they rarely procrastinate. As someone once said, *"The best way to get something done is to begin."*

Have you ever encountered a time when you needed to do something, but it was hard for you to get started? But later on, after starting, you realized it wasn't a hard task after all?

The law of inertia states that *an object at rest will remain at rest.* So, if you don't start then nothing will happen. On the contrary, the law of motion also states that *an object in motion remains in motion.*

So if you want to do something, start doing it. Do it immediately, because later on, you will realize how unstoppable you are once you're moving.

So, friend, "take action," because "You are a highly successful person."

## 6. Life-Long Learner

Have you ever heard the word *"Kaizen"?* It is a Japanese word meaning "continuous improvement." Did you know that successful people always grow themselves, always improve themselves, and always make themselves better?

Thomas Corley studied rich people and poor people regarding the learning habits which they cultivate every day. Here is the breakdown:

- 88% of self-made millionaires read for learning every day vs. 2% of the poor

- 86% of these millionaires love to read vs. 26% of the poor

- 11% of these millionaires read for entertainment vs. 79% of the poor

Do you see the difference? Rich, successful people make it a habit to learn something every day. They learn to improve themselves, to grow themselves, and to nurture themselves, every single day.

Be a life-long learner, friend, because "You are a highly successful person."

## 7. Passion

Successful people are passionate about what they do. Let's look at some examples of successful people we know about:

Bill Gates: Did you know that long before he became the founder of Microsoft, he was an amateur programmer who was passionate about computers? So passionate, in fact, that in eighth grade he managed to get excused from math class so he could design things like early video games.

Walt Disney: Do you know how Disney spent his time while growing up? Well, working -- but also drawing, from an early age. Yes, he was pretty young when he sold his first drawing (of a neighbor's horse).

Warren Buffet: One time, on ESPN's *Mike & Mike* radio show, Buffett was asked what the underlying secret to his almost immeasurable success was. Do you know what he said?

*"I found what I love to do very early. When I was seven or eight years old I knew that this particular game really, really intrigued me. And then I had some great teachers along the way."*

Yes, friend, these are highly successful people who follow what they love to do, who follow their passions.

Remember, you only have one life to live, so do the things you love. Do the things that excite you. Do the things that make you feel alive. Do what your heart wants you to do. Follow your passion.

Again, friend, remember: you only have one life to live. Do what you love because "You are a highly successful person."

## 8. Positive Mental Attitude

Successful people have a positive mental attitude. They have a can-do attitude. They believe in themselves, always think positively, always say positive things, and ignore negative people who discourage them. They associate themselves with highly successful, positive, nurturing people.

In the book *Think and Grow Rich*, by Napoleon Hill, the concept of positive mental attitude was first developed and introduced. He emphasizes the importance of positive thinking as a principle to success. This has always been one of the key secrets of successful people.

Truly, this is one of *the* most important characteristics of highly successful people.

As Zig Ziglar says, *"Positive thinking will let you do everything better than negative thinking will."*

So, always think positively, act positively, and believe in yourself. Remember, you already have everything you need inside of you. You just have to believe in yourself.

Once again, friend, always have a positive mental attitude towards everything, because "You are a highly successful person."

## 9. Value Provider

Some of you may be asking, "Andrian, what do you mean by that?" I will tell you: successful people are value providers. They are problem solvers who solve many of society's problems.

Want proof? Bill Gates. What does he provide? Microsoft (computers, software, etc.). Yes, a large percentage of people in the world use Microsoft. Maybe you are one of them.

Then there's Mark Zuckerberg. What does he provide? Facebook (easy communication, instant networking, etc.).

As a successful person, you need to provide value. You need to solve problems. You need to be a solution provider.

What do you think you can do to provide value to people? Think about it.

Maybe it has something to do with your talents, your skills, your knowledge, or even your time. Look at your strengths, and ask yourself, "What value can I provide to people?" "How can I help other people?"

The more people you help, the more blessings you will receive.

Remember to always provide value because "You are a highly successful person."

## 10. Consistency

Have you ever heard of Larry Bird, the NBA Hall of Famer? Do you want to know one of the secrets of his success?

Here it is: He got up early in the morning to shoot 500 free throws – EVERY day.

Yes, you read that right. Every day. And because of that daily consistency, he has one of the highest free throw averages in the NBA (88.6%). Because of that consistency, he is now in the NBA Hall of Fame.

I can almost hear you saying, *"Wow!"* It's amazing, isn't it?

It seems when you do something daily, even little things, in the long run, it will have a huge impact on your life.

What do you think you can do today – consistently, every day – which can have a huge impact on your life? Is it building an online business? Is it reading a great book for 20 minutes each day? Is it watching the stock market every day? Is it playing the piano? Is it writing an article every single day? Whatever it is, friend, do it every day – consistently.

This is one of the most powerful characteristics of highly successful people – the compounding effect of their daily habits.

Try it. Do it daily – consistently – and after a year or two, you will notice how much you've grown, how successful you've been, and what a different person you've become.

Remember, friend, consistency is the key, because "You are a highly successful person."

## 11. Big Dreamer

As Brian Tracy says, "*All successful people, men and women, are big dreamers. They imagine what their future could be, ideal in every respect, and then they walk every day toward their distant vision, that goal or purpose.*"

Successful people dream big. Successful people think big. Successful people believe big. Successful people expect big.

Friend, all of the successful people that we know have the habit of thinking big.

Michael Jordan dreamed of becoming a basketball superstar. He is now considered *the greatest basketball player of all time.*

Tiger Woods dreamed of becoming the world's best golfer. He is now considered *the greatest golfer of all time.*

Bill Gates dreamed of a computer in every home around the world. And, as of this writing, he is considered *the wealthiest man in the world.*

These are some of the most highly successful people that we know about. And they all have something in common: they are *big dreamers.*

So friend, always dream big, always think big, because "You are a highly successful person."

Just to recap, here are the 11 characteristics of highly successful people:

1. Focus

2. 'Push Yourself Out of Your Comfort Zone' Attitude

3. Persistence

4. Goal-Oriented

5. Action-Taker

6. Life-Long Learner

7. Passion

8. Positive Mental Attitude

9. Value Provider

10. Consistency

11. Big Dreamer

And before I end this chapter, I would like to share with you a beautiful quote from David Brooks:

*"Almost every successful person begins with two beliefs:*

*"The future can be better than the present.*

*"And I have the power to make it so."*

Friend, always remember that, you already have everything you need to become a highly successful person. It's already inside of you – because "You are a highly successful person."

# POSITIVE ENERGY POWER #9: HAPPINESS – HOW TO LIVE A HAPPY LIFE EVERY DAY (IS THAT POSSIBLE?)

Have you ever asked yourself, "How can I live a happy life every day?" Is it even really possible? Is there really a technique or strategy on how to live a happy life every day? Or is there a principle or law that we can follow to live a happy life every day?

In this last chapter, I'll share a few techniques and tips on how to really live a happy life every day.

One of the best books I've read about happiness is *Being Happy,* by Andrew Matthews.

What I really like about the book is that it tackles more about the human mind. The human mind can be compared to an iceberg.

The tip of the iceberg, which we can see, is the conscious part of the brain. The bigger part of the iceberg, which we don't usually see, is the subconscious.

The subconscious mind is the quiet part of the brain which records our thoughts, habits, memories, and which also influences our actions. More often than not, the things we experience in life, especially the behaviors that keep coming back, are caused by the subconscious mind.

You may be thinking, "So, Andrian, what does that have to do with our happiness?"

Well, in order to live a happy life every day, we need to put happy, positive, nurturing, inspirational, and motivational thoughts into our conscious and subconscious mind. Some of you may be asking, "Andrian, how can I do that?"

In this chapter, I'm going to show you the secrets of the happiest people in the world. This is also a great way to wrap up the entire book.

## Here Are The 6 Ways To Live A Happy Life Every Day:

### 1. Gratitude

One of the secrets of the happiest people I know is that they are always thankful for everything they have, whether they have it in abundance or not.

Anthony Robbins once said, *"The antidote to fear is gratitude. The antidote to anger is gratitude. You can't feel fear or anger while feeling gratitude at the same time."*

Yes, being filled with gratitude for everything can really have a great impact on our lives. Why? Because once we feel grateful for everything, we will naturally feel good.

Try this simple technique right now: Think of three things which you are grateful for right this moment. For example, your smartphone, the Internet, the food you eat, or even the clothes you are wearing right now. Say *"thank you"* for them. Doesn't that feel good? Yup, it does.

So my advice is that when you feel sad, discouraged, angry, or any other negative feeling, try to think about the things you are grateful for and your mind will wander to other good, positive things in your life. You will definitely feel better.

## 2. Forgiveness

Mahatma Gandhi once said, *"The weak can never forgive. Forgiveness is the attribute of the strong."*

Are you strong? Do you hold a grudge in your heart toward someone? Is it really difficult for you to forgive?

Yes, I know it's difficult and really hard to do. But do you know when you're not forgiving, you're only hurting yourself over and over again, while the one who has hurt you is maybe sitting on the beach, enjoying life, and totally clueless about the pain and hurt you feel?

So, now, *"let's be STRONG,"* as Mahatma Gandhi stated above. You may be thinking, "Andrian, I want to forgive. I want to be strong. I just don't know how to forgive. How do I do that?"

I'm going to tell you a simple technique that I've been using for years.

Forgiveness takes place in your *mind*. There is no need for you to go personally to someone to forgive him or her. You can do it right here, right now, using only your mind. (The only time you would need to forgive someone in person would be if they came to you, asking for your forgiveness.)

Once someone has done something to me that's not good or that I've been hurt by, and it keeps on repeating over and over again in my mind, this is what I do:

*I close my eyes and imagine the person who has wronged me as if I'm talking to him face to face. I say, "I'm hurt by what you said/did (be specific), but I know you said/did that because (try to look at their perspective as objectively as you can). I would like to say I'm sorry if I've done something to offend you.*

*Today, right now, I'm choosing to forgive you. I'm now forgiving you. I'm now releasing you. And I'm now free. I'm now free."*

From then on, my mind is in *blessing mode*. My mind is now ready to receive peace and blessings. As the Bible says in Romans 12:14, *"bless and do not curse."* Go ahead and try the technique outlined above and "be strong." You will feel peace and happiness continually come into your life every single day. The more you forgive, the more you'll feel peaceful inside.

You can do this every day, even with the small irritations that come your way. I know this is really effective. Remember, friend, it's all in your *mind*, so it's better to overcome it in your mind.

### 3. Love Yourself

Someone once said, *"You cannot give what you do not have."* I believe that's definitely true. You cannot give an apple to someone if you don't have an apple. You cannot give love to someone if you don't have love to give.

The question now is: "How can we love ourselves?"

Here are some ways we can love ourselves more:

a) **Have "me" time.** Have time for yourself, alone. No distractions, no social media, no responsibilities, no phones, no calls – just you, alone. During this time, think and reflect on what's happening in your life right now.

Create a strategy. Make a plan to achieve your dreams. Go somewhere quiet where you can think well. Go to the beach. Go for a drive in the country. Go to the mountains. Read a book that inspires you. Just give yourself a break. You deserve it. This will definitely fill up your "love tank."

b) **Forgive yourself.** Yes, you might stumble sometimes, but learn to forgive yourself. We all make mistakes, and we all fail at times in our lives.

It's not good to be eaten up by guilt, condemnation, or regrets. Forgive yourself. Ask God to forgive you, confess your sins to Him. God says in Proverbs 28:13 (NKJV), *"He who covers his sins will not prosper, but whoever confesses and forsakes them will have mercy."*

Remember that God is always ready to forgive you, once you *ask*. So forgive yourself more often, and always say to yourself, *"I'm going to do better next time."*

c) **Do what you love.** Remember, you have talents and skills which other people don't have. You are the only person who can do what you can do. So do the things that you love.

Do things which make you feel alive. Follow your passion. If you love writing, then write. If you love dancing, then dance. If you love swimming, then swim. You have your talents and skills for a reason. Use them to nurture the world around you and inspire people.

But most importantly, do it because you love doing it, not because someone else wants you to do it. Have the freedom to live out your passions. Be the best you can be.

d) **Grow yourself.** Jim Rohn says, *"If you want to have more, you have to become more. For things to change, you have to change. For things to get better, you have to get better. For things to improve, you have to improve. If you grow, everything grows for you."* He's right!

You need to grow yourself. I know you have dreams and goals. Pursue them. Before you can achieve them, you have to "become more." How? Read books about self-improvement, read the biographies of other successful people, listen to audio/video podcasts that motivate, inspire, and encourage you to become a better person.

Attend seminars and training sessions which cultivate your mind and make you grow. Remember, if you grow, everything grows for you.

Those are just a few of the ways you can love yourself more. Again, friend, love yourself and live a happy life every day.

## 4. Associate with Happy and Positive People

As Jack Canfield says, *"One of the things I tell people in my seminars is to hang out with positive, nurturing people. You become like who you hang out with."*

In order to live a happy life every day, you need to associate yourself with positive, nurturing, happy people. You cannot be with someone who's always complaining, always sad, or always seeing the negative side of things and expect yourself to be happy. Don't allow yourself to be dragged down by the people you associate with.

Find people who are happy and positive, who encourage you and have a deep sense of life. Remember, you always have a choice. Each day you can make a decision about who you will associate with.

If you feel the person you spend most of your time with is dragging you down, or if you feel discouraged or down every time you're with that person, consider this, friend: Their negative attitude may wear off on you. Do you really want that to happen?

Be wise; choose your associates wisely. Always be with happy, positive, and enthusiastic people. These are the people who are there to support you, to encourage you, to motivate you, to inspire you, and to nurture you.

Associate with people who have big dreams, who have a "can-do" attitude, who are optimistic and excited about life, and who have a deep sense of purpose in life.

These are the people who will help you achieve your dreams, who will encourage you when you are down, who will be with you in your success, and who will teach you how to live life.

Choose wisely, friend, and live a happy life every day.

## 5. Give

One of the best quotes I have ever heard or read is by Anthony Robbins:

*"The secret to living is giving."*

This is truly one of the secrets to a happy life: giving.

The LORD Jesus Himself said in Acts 20:35, *"It is more blessed to give than to receive."*

When you give, you naturally feel happy. Because when you give, you produce a chemical in your brain called *serotonin* which is associated with feeling happy.

In fact, a survey was done of more than 3,000 volunteers of all ages which documented the physical and emotional benefits of giving. A full 50% reported feeling a "helper's high" after helping someone. Other studies have shown that those who give to others experience increased health and happiness.

There you have it, friend. In order to live a happy life every day, give as often as you can. Give to the needy. Give to the poor. Give to charity. Give more to your church, above and beyond your tithe. Give generously.

Proverbs 11:25 states, *"A generous person will prosper; whoever refreshes others will be refreshed."* So, give more, and live a happy life.

## 6. Get Enough Restful Sleep

Yes, sleep. That's number six on my list. Why? Because study after study confirms that the more sleep you get, the happier you tend to be. Awesome!

I know, some of us find it extremely hard to get to sleep early; you need to catch up with your favorite TV show, with the news, with the ball game, or you need to socialize with your friends on Facebook, Twitter, Instagram or Pinterest, and so on.

I'm sure you've noticed that the later you go to sleep at night, the harder it is to get up in the morning. And then you're late, so you need to rush through breakfast, getting dressed, and driving to work, only to arrive late at work and have your boss watching you. Then your whole day seems to be hurried, and you feel so negative, like you don't have enough energy. Then after work, you drive back home and do the same thing all over again. This cycle must be stopped!

Sleep is the answer. Yes, sleep! Get some rest. Sleep at least 7-8 hours every day. This changes your mood in the morning. You will notice when you have enough restful sleep, you feel invigorated, energized, happy, excited, positive, and overall great. And I assure you your whole day will be great.

So get to sleep early, and live a happy life every day.

There you have it, friend. The six keys to being happy every day. Just as a recap, here they are again:

1. Gratitude

2. Forgiveness

3. Love Yourself

4. Associate with Happy and Positive People

5. Give

6. Get Enough Restful Sleep

Oh, and this is the best part! Did you know there's *one ultimate secret to happiness*? I've discovered it, and I want to share it with you. For me, this is *the* greatest secret to Happiness:

*"My relationship with GOD."*

Now, some of you might be saying, "Andrian, you're a religious person, so you have to say that. I'm not religious, and I'd rather not think about such things."

But you know what, friend? This is the real secret to happiness in the world. After I came to know Jesus Christ and surrendered my life to Him, and after I let Him be my LORD and Savior, I've found the true and real meaning of happiness.

This is *not* about religion. This is about *"relationship."* You might know about God and maybe even believe in God, but do you have a personal relationship with Him?

A real relationship with God is similar to a relationship with a friend. You have face-to-face conversations and communicate intimately, just like with your friend.

A relationship with God is the same. You can talk to God the same way you talk to your friend. God talks to you through His Word, the Bible, or through another believer, or through the circumstances you're going through.

Friend, always remember that *"God loves you."*

I believe it's no accident that you are reading this book. There's a reason why God put this book into your hands: to hear these words, to read these words. You know why, friend?

Because *"God loves you."*

Friend, if you want to have a personal relationship with God, and you want to surrender everything to Him – your life, your burdens, your problems, your finances, your relationships, your health, whatever it may be – just follow me in this prayer:

*"LORD, I know it's not an accident that I am reading this book right now. I know there's a reason why You brought me to this point. LORD, I believe my life is meaningless without You. I want to have true peace, true happiness, and true joy in my life. I understand that I can only have that when I'm in a relationship with You. I want that – a personal relationship with You. Today, LORD Jesus, forgive me from all the things I've done, from all my sins and wrongdoings. I repent. I believe in You. I believe You died on the cross for me, to save me so that I may have everlasting life with You. Today, LORD Jesus, I accept You as my LORD and Savior. Starting today, I surrender my life to You and let You take full control. In Jesus' name, Amen."*

If you prayed that prayer or something along those lines, "CONGRATULATIONS, FRIEND!" You are now on your journey to true peace, true happiness, and true joy with Jesus Christ. That's the real secret to live a happy life every day.

# "THANK YOU, FRIEND."

Here we are at the end of this book. I believe you have gained lots of insight, knowledge, and wisdom from this book which you can apply in your own life. If you do, you too can live a positive life every day.

Again, I want to say *thank you*, my friend, for joining me on this journey called "life."

In this book, together, we have learned about the importance of a positive life: how to think positively; how to gain confidence and self-esteem; the top secret morning habits of successful people; how to motivate ourselves every single day; how to use the power of prayer to achieve what we want in life; how forgiveness can change our lives; how gratitude can benefit us in many ways; the real characteristics of highly successful people; and finally about how to live a happy life every day.

Truly, these are the keys and powers of a positive life.

I'm so excited for you, my friend. I hope you'll be able to apply all the learning, knowledge, insights and wisdom of this book into your life.

## A Quick Favor, Friend.

I would like to ask for less than a minute of your time, friend. Would you please share this book to your Facebook account so that your friends and family can also read it? Always remember: If even one person reads this book because of your recommendation, you will have made a big difference in his/her life. Think of the happiness and joy you will feel knowing you have made a difference in someone's life. I want you to experience that, so I'm giving you this opportunity and the link below so you can share this book with your family and friends on Facebook: **www.bit.ly/ilovepositiveenergy**

Or, you may also buy copies of this book on Amazon, and give them as a birthday or Christmas gift to family and friends. It makes a great gift!

With that, I want to thank you for your love and support. Your decision to buy this book shows you are a life-changer. I'm very proud of you, friend.

Also, friend, please share your love by leaving a 5-star and positive review on Amazon. As always, your love and support are highly appreciated. Here's the Amazon link so you can easily leave a positive review on Amazon:

**www.bit.ly/ReviewPositiveEnergy**

I truly appreciate your love and support, friend, and I'm happy because you're happy. :)

Always remember, friend:

"*By changing our thinking, we change our lives.*"

"The Power of Positive Energy: Powerful Thinking, Powerful Life"

Your friend,

Andrian Teodoro

# Your Free Gift

As a way of saying *thanks* for your purchase of this book, I'm offering a free eBook called *Abundant Thinking: Achieving the Rich Dad Mindset* that's exclusive to my book readers.

In *Abundant Thinking: Achieving the Rich Dad Mindset,* you'll discover how to become an abundant thinker. This means you'll no longer fall into the trap of 'lack mindset.' You will also learn the power of The Law of Abundance, how to practice Abundant Thinking in your life, the power of Abundance Motivation, 15 ways to be an Abundant Thinker, and the 'Top 10 Secrets' of having a Rich Dad Mindset. This means you will be more successful and happier in life.

Get your free copy of *Abundant Thinking: Achieving the Rich Dad Mindset* at:

**www.bit.ly/AbundantThinkingFree**

# ALSO FROM ANDRIAN TEODORO

*The Power of Positive Energy: Powerful Thinking, Powerful Life Audiobook*

*(Available on Audible, Amazon, and iTunes)*

*The Power of Positive Energy: Powerful Thinking, Powerful Life Kindle version*

*(Available on Amazon)*

# RESOURCES AND BOOKS HIGHLY RECOMMENDED BY THE AUTHOR

*Think and Grow Rich,* by Napoleon Hill

*The Power of Positive Thinking,* by Norman Vincent Peale

*The Magic of Thinking Big,* by David Schwartz

*Your Best Life Now,* by Joel Osteen

*How to Win Friends and Influence People,* by Dale Carnegie

*The 21 Irrefutable Laws of Leadership,* by John Maxwell

*Rich Dad, Poor Dad,* by Robert Kiyosaki

*Secrets of the Millionaire Mind,* by T.Harv Eker

*As a Man Thinketh,* by James Allen

*The Seven Spiritual Laws of Success,* by Deepak Chopra

*The 7 Habits of Highly Effective People,* by Stephen Covey

*The Greatest Salesman in the World,* by Og Mandino

*Don't Sweat the Small Stuff,* by Richard Carlson

*Awaken the Giant Within,* by Anthony Robbins

*See You at the Top,* by Zig Ziglar

*Being Happy,* by Andrew Matthews

*How to Simplify Your Life,* by Tiki Kustenmacher

# About the Author

## *Andrian Teodoro*

Andrian Teodoro is a highly motivational speaker and Christian author like Joel Osteen, John Maxwell, Rick Warren, Joseph Prince, Zig Ziglar, Joyce Meyer and Terri Savelle Foy. His mission is to enlighten, motivate, inspire, and help others to make a quality, happy, peaceful, positive, and fulfilled life. His passion and hobbies revolve around personal development. He loves to read great books, listen to audio/video materials, and attend training and seminars about personal development, mindset, financial freedom, time freedom, business, entrepreneurship, leadership, motivation, spiritual retreats and success.

Andrian is a very optimistic person. His favorite subjects are about positive mind, positive thinking, and positive thoughts. He really believes that everything starts with a thought.

He has a quote that says *"If you start the day right, your whole day will be bright."*

Andrian is a Christian, and many of the principles in his book come from the Book of Truth - the Bible.

This is one of his favorite verses in the Bible,

*"As [a man] thinks in his heart, so is he."*

Proverbs 23:7 (NKJV)

He always believes that:

*"Life is beautiful."* and *"With God all things are possible."*

Made in the USA
Middletown, DE
06 April 2018